CW00693626

Bernard,

Can you still <u>still</u>
squeeze through
the railings?

Joe.

I Remember

Reflections on Fishing in Childhood

compiled by

Joe Cowley

SUMMERSDALE

Summersdale Publishers
46 West Street
Chichester
West Sussex
PO19 1RP
England

A CIP catalogue record for this book is available from
the British Library.

Printed and bound in Great Britain
by Selwood Printing Ltd, Burgess Hill.

ISBN 1 873475 43 8

All royalties from the sale of this book will be donated
to the NSPCC.

Acknowledgements

To the following artists who suffered my pesterings and who contributed their work at very short notice.

Barry Appleby - Steve Colgan - Laura Cowley - Steve Fisher - Lynn McKenna - Richard Pooley - Michael Pugh - Edward Robinson - Paul Sample (cover) - Michael Thomas - Graham Thompson - Carl Waine - Ivan Wilding.

Alastair Williams and Stewart Ferris - publishers who have supported this cause.

Permissions

A Marvel of Caddis was first published by Cassell in "The Angler's Sedge" by Taff Price.

"Scouse Mouse" by George Melly was first published by Weidenfield and Nicholson.

These publishers have very generously waived their usual fee.

Summersdale Publishers gratefully acknowledge the authors for their permission to publish these stories in this volume. The copyright for each story remains the property of the author concerned.

Dedication:

To Old Father Thames - he taught me much.

Contents

Foreword

By Giles Pegram,
Appeals Director of the NSPCC

I have been told, and no doubt you will know this to be true, that fishing is one of the biggest leisure pursuits in the country. I hope that this fact is correct and that those of you who pick up this book not only like to fish but also like to read about fishing.

All the contributors have generously given their time and their recollections free of charge in the hope that their pleasure will raise money for the NSPCC's work with abused and neglected children. The NSPCC relies heavily on the generosity of the public to fund its 144 projects and centres throughout England, Wales and Northern Ireland. Children First undertake a similar role in Scotland.

You can be sure that if you purchase this book you will spend time immersed in people's happy memories of the first time they went fishing or telling tales about the one that got away. This may seem a small price to pay for the incidental pleasure of helping to protect and prevent cruelty to children.

Introduction

By Joe Cowley

Fortunately, I was on good terms with a fellow pupil of my school who knew all the wrinkles of life from an early age. The snob in me wondered how he had got into Ealing Grammar School but I was glad that he was there. He let me in on the secret of where to write for the licence granted only to the few.

Her Majesty approved my application and eventually her postman arrived with the precious document. I was now at liberty to "angle with rod and line" in the Royal Parks. The bountiful waters of Hampton Court, Richmond Great Park and Osterley Park were my oysters. The great day arrived: with seal of approval tucked securely about my person, it was off to Osterley for me. I mounted my trusty "Gamages Youth's cycle" and pedalled off from South Ealing towards the grandly named Great West Road. I was used to the altered aerodynamics of my machine for such trips with rods secured along the crossbar, saddlebag stuffed with enough egg and bacon sandwiches to open a caff, rucksack bulging with tackle to cover every conceivable eventuality and keepnet swinging dangerously close to the spokes. My wellies did not quite fit the toe-clips but this was not a race.

The cycle track made for a smooth and safe ride; I was soon turning into the pot-holed, bum jarring drive that led to my reed-fringed goal. As it came into view I realised that I had never seen such an ideal water. A large irregular shaped expanse; I was spoilt for choice by so many inviting swims. My youthful idealism persuaded me that the absence of fellow anglers was due to the exclusivity of the location. This really was a dream come true - I had stepped into the pages of "Mr Crabtree Goes Fishing". Once again he would be proving to his son that he was the perfect dad; surely the smoke from his pipe would start to curl above those nearby reeds.

I was happy just to be there - lost in the concentration of mind on red point of quill float below the tip of my trusty bamboo rod. There were certain to be vast shoals of fish cruising ever closer.

Having spent most of the day catching a few voracious perch and a couple of stunted rudd, I decided to concentrate on the specimen bream. The other angler present had kindly revealed where those slab-sided monsters could be found. Armed with this confidential information, I set off through the undergrowth until I arrived in a remote clearing opposite an island. Imagining the tell-tale bubbles of fish feeding against the far bank, I set up the appropriate tackle. Well it was the best I had. My mother, who travelled far and wide, had presented me with some technically advanced equipment from Canada: however unsuitable a solid glass, single-handed, five foot rod with closed-face reel was, its casting power was magic. My bait simply flew to the island. A crude ping-pong ball size piece of bread paste was my sensitive bite detector.

Darkness came and with it the rain. Stair rods and cats and dogs combined to dampen my enthusiasm: they failed.

Two problems were now to be overcome. Even at the age of thirteen I was not keen on a dark bedroom never mind the pitch black outdoors - on my own. Also, I was somewhat concerned about the risk of incarceration in The Tower for fishing after sunset. Defensively, I concentrated on the dough ball, the consistency of which was strong enough to withstand the monsoon. There it hung, bathed in the narrow beam of white light piercing forward from my gently steaming bike lamp. The embryo loaf trembled slightly each time that it was struck by an extra-large raindrop: otherwise it hung motionless.

Suddenly it happened - the indicator rocketed skyward as the line jerked taught - quick as lightning the rod was in my hands. The bream gave a realistic impression of a wet sack as it bid for freedom. However, I was convinced that this was a spirited fight that needed all my skills to bring fish to net. The multi-purpose lamp picked out a specimen of about 11/2 pounds. If I'm honest, the passage of time has probably increased the true figure.

Contrary to all rules and regulations I kept the fish as proof of my prowess. My sense of right and wrong was overwhelmed by my sense of achievement as the now expired trophy was wrapped in a damp shroud to be borne ceremoniously home. I packed hurriedly and squelched back to my trusty steed waiting patiently by the railings. Loading for the return journey was not as systematic as the inward leg; I reached the main road with rods protruding at all angles; the rucksack making a determined bid to unseat me; and I was soaked. My socks had removed themselves from my feet within the confines of my wellies.

Uncomfortable but elated I arrived home. The monster fish had shrunk in my saddlebag but in triumph I tipped it into the kitchen sink - Ma would be proud. The bream was a fighter to the last. Finding a new lease of life it started to flap and slap against the cold, dry porcelain. The next few minutes were a blur of blind panic: Oh my God what had I done; what will Ma say; what will Her Majesty say!

To this day I feel shame for the way that I concealed my treasonable act. Oblivious to the slime, I seized the brave, gasping fish and ran straight to the dustbin. I stuffed it down, amongst the eggshells, potato peelings and last week's newspapers and slammed on the lid. The resounding clang from the galvanised coffin would surely have reverberated all the way up The Mall and echoed through the corridors of Buckingham Palace.

My mother looked up from her typewriter.

"Had a good day?"

"Not bad."

"Did you catch anything?"

"Just a few small ones."

Standing in the shadow beyond the glare of the table lamp, my guilty face was hidden as I blurted,

"I put them all back."

The busy thudding of the machine resumed as I left the room to begin the rest of my life burdened with my secret.

I can recall that day in minute detail and wallow in the vivid memory. I can derive pleasure from it. This is in stark contrast to the memories of those abused in their formative years who either have to live with the recollection or suffer by trying to exclude the pictures.

My brief to contributors to this book was to write about anything connected with fish or fishing as or with children - as simple as that. All authors donated their work to this anthology which is being sold to raise funds for The National Society for the Prevention of Cruelty to Children. Many of them lead hectic lives and I thank them for taking time and trouble to write. A few of the items are fiction but most are very real and strong images reflecting the warmth of growing up and learning about fishing - especially with or as a father. About time a few more mums got out there.

In the natural course of relating angling experiences many have gone beyond their childhood and on into youth and later years: an indication that little boys never grow up. But we remain parents and children for many years don't we? The real truth of the matter is that the time spent in big game fishing in some exotic gulf pales into insignificance against the golden memory of those first fish from some humble stream or pond - part of the magic of angling.

A few of the pieces are written by children of Lessness Heath School, Belvedere in Kent. As often is the case they present some perfectly clear and straightforward views on fishing. Fish provide a subject for simple verse.

Some of these reminiscences suggest that many of us are indebted to a surrogate angling father: Mr Crabtree. Oh how we yearned to be his son - to climb into those black and white drawings. We certainly learned from Bernard Venables' books. I had to correct one or two authors unable to recall Crabtree Junior's name - Peter.

You too can learn from this book: practical lessons; how to encourage young anglers; how catching fish doesn't always matter. Many of the experiences will seem familiar. Take pleasure from the warmth of that sensation. Enjoy this book and encourage non-anglers to read it - you will be surprised how many of the uninitiated will appreciate it.

I must give special thanks to Charles Jardine for his initial encouragement and continuing advice - to Bernard Cribbins for his enthusiasm and suggestions in the early stages. Finally to the artists who worked to a very tight deadline to provide a wide variety of fine illustrations. Please take time out to study the detail and appreciate the eye-aching effort that has created each piece.

If you have purchased this book then you have also contributed to much needed funds. If you have borrowed it: donations are always welcome.

Simple Truths

By Bernard Venables

If I were called upon by parents to bestow a blessing on their son, newly brought to life in this world, a blessing that could go with him for the length of his life, what should it be? The answer needs little thought: of course, of course; let the lad be an angler, on the face of it no more need be said.

But only on the face of it. In former times just that would have been ample to ensure a life rich with sensitive delights - only in our time, our recent time, have there come elements that, seeming to be devised only for the soonest and greatest success for him, in the outcome deprive him.

The true pleasures of angling are of privacy - something that is like a small light glowing in the mind whatever the outward world is demanding, something that goes with its owner like a secret friend. It is to be wished for the boy who comes to angling that he is not too well advantaged: if he shall have some difficulty in finding water for his fishing, that is probably to his advantage. Probably too it is better that tackle shall not come easily to him. If he must save earnestly, or improvise, for his tackle, the man he becomes will think himself to have been fortunate. For the fullest happiness of the boy, he should have an interval of longing. The world being as it is now it cannot really be expected of the boy that he must start with a garden cane and a bent pin, as was usually the case in my time; but at least let him start with one cheap rod and the simplest of reels. To smother him with easily come-by and sophisticated tackle is to deprive him. It denies him that magical path of gradual discovery which should be his.

Let us look instead at the beginnings of those of my generation - indeed the beginnings of all generations until the last few decades. But for simplicity let it be just my progress. I was born with a haunting awareness of water and the bewitchment of the life within it. Its spell was the greater because the only water open to me - minor ponds - were opaque, green. Imagine then the mystery of that; what unseen creatures had their being beneath that surface? I, as would any boy, pictured them in my mind's eye, silent, gliding, with jewelled eyes, fish, alive. So strong was the vision that long failure intensified it. Far from failure inducing loss of faith it made it the more compelling. First little successes when they did come brought ecstasy.

When nowadays I see the angling press boys pictured with massive carp caught not with skill acquired by long and lovely apprenticeship, but with a devilry of electronic gadgetry of great cost, I remember the tender triumphs of the past. Poor boys, I think, poor lads; are any of the old delights left for them now? The true pleasures of fishing have been bludgeoned out of their reach by such gross and easy success.

After those earliest days of murky ponds I progressed to first rivers, minor ones, of no famous glory. No great barbel could they offer, no fat chub under the willows. Roach, if just sometimes they did come, were trophies of great joy if they could nudge the spring balance near the half-pound. But what intense days of bliss those were, often in a heaven of loneliness because then rivers were still uncrowded. The air of those water meadows was soft; its breezes carried the scent of the river before even it was reached. Then there it was, dank, lovely with promise. Alders leaned over the current that slipped beguilingly against the undercut bank. There were secret-looking holes in the elbows of the river's bends that even the boy inexperienced as I knew could mean bristling hordes of perch.

And then I had no pricey rod of some chemist's concoction, no reel so clever that it could almost think. My stiff old rod and even stiffer reel were very difficult for casting: I learnt a lot about sorting tangles, easing the line out of the branches. And I had a lovely time; the happiness of it all was great. When in time I progressed to a reel that was not stiff, which ran with silky smoothness, I had to learn the elegant art of using it - casting with the centre-pin reel. I would have the boy starter of today confined at first to the centre-pin reel because I would want him to miss none of the pleasures of fishing. When he had become secure in his skill with the centre-pin, then I would allow him to come to the fixed-spool reel because that has much usefulness for some purposes. But it is easy to use, too easy, too corrupting for a boy early in his growing to be a skilled and therefore, contented angler.

The heart of the intense pleasure of fishing is not the catching of fish, just that. That is one part of the pleasure. Nor does it lie in the catching of very big fish, red letter fish. That is part of it too; we all hope to catch big fish. But it is the nature of fishing that it can give its happiness when we are not catching fish at all - greatly as we all hope to. The skill we use in the catching of fish is an important part of the pleasure - the fluent casting of float tackle or the delicate presenting of a fly before a rising fish. Finally and perhaps the most enchanting element of all - the places where we fish.

Yes, to give the boy, new-coming to this world, the best blessing he could have, I would have him an angler. But I think it very important indeed that he should start the right way.

The Tench

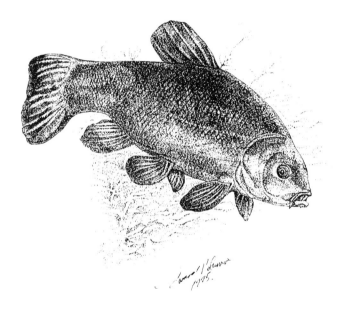

By Frederick Forsyth

The sun was shining, the sky was blue. As well they might be, for it was June the 16th and the season for coarse fishing had just begun.

So I went to the cupboard and got out my trusty twelve-foot Shakespeare float rod and dusty tackle box, unused these many years since I had last been to a lake or canal in pursuit of the bream, the roach the barbel and the carp.

"Wossat?" said Shane who was just then turned three.

"A fishing rod, silly," said Stuart, about to be five. "Are we going fishing?"

"Yeh," said Shane and did a small war dance, finally colliding with a bookcase bringing down a rack of Ladybird volumes depicting the adventures of such notables as Billy Goat Gruff and Chicken Little.

The tackle box was in a parlous state, but eventually I managed to put together a reel and spare, enough line, weights, floats and hooks to make up several rigs to carry us through the day.

"The next thing we need," I announced portentously, "is bait."

"Bait," said Shane and did another small dance until subdued by his elder brother. It was a long way to go to the nearest tackle shop from Frensham, but an acre of garden beckoned outside the windows, so I collected a shovel from the potting shed and went to look for worms.

Worm hunting took an hour and the worms that were not used for insertion into collars went into a Tupperware container from the kitchen. Supplementary rations in the form of orangeade and biscuits went into the same haversack, a small stool was collected from the summerhouse and finally we were ready for some serious business with the inhabitants of the Cut Mill Pond at Elstead.

There were hardly any pegs left when we got there, the best hot-spots having been taken by those arriving before dawn. But at last I found one - a hole in the undergrowth of the lake's bank, beneath some overhanging trees. There was no chance of an overhead cast; an underhand would have to do, with a final flick to carry the baited hook, weights and float out of the shadows and into the sunlit water beyond the trees.

Watched by four saucer eyes, I tested the depth of the water, shortening the distance between the lowest of the lead weights and the float until finally the slim piece of bright cork bobbed upright and nodded merrily among the ripples.

Eight feet was the depth from surface to mud, so I set the float at seven feet above the hook and prepared the bait. The boys watched agog as a plump pink worm was nicked just behind the head and consigned, wriggling furiously, to his watery grave. Out on the sunlit lake the bright orange head of the float settled, straightened and became still.

"What happens now?" whispered Stuart.

"We wait." I said. "Somewhere down there a fish will find the worm, have it for lunch and then we pull it in."

Small boys have a rather short attention span, and within ten minutes Shane was away exploring the undergrowth. Stuart stuck it out for a bit longer.

Lunch passed in an orgy of biscuits and orangeade, followed by complaints that this was a very boring way of spending a day. Just after one, the float bobbed, recovered and dunked again.

"Pssst," I said, "something's there."

They came out of the bushes and watched the bobbing float.

"Fishy," whispered Shane.

"Pull it in, Dad," suggested Stuart.

"Not yet. . . . he hasn't made up his mind yet."

The fish did so even as I spoke. The float did one last quick bob, then dived at a slant, the bright colour fading away in the bronze-tinted water. I flicked the rod tip upward to make the strike, felt the thud and the pause, then the steady strain as the line pulled away towards deep water. The rod tip bent over like a hairpin and the line ran out.

I was using 5lb test line and set the slipping clutch on the open-face reel to half that. Whatever fish was down there did not bother about two and a half pounds - the line ran out and out until the fish was back in the centre of the Cut Mill. Shane, in T-shirt, short pants and chubby legs in bright blue wellies, jumped up and down and yelled to everyone else: "We got a fishy."

Stuart, older and more serious, studied the straining rod and the line. Slowly, I worked the fish back towards the rod, then gave the rod to Stuart.

I could tell it was not a bad fish, and thought they would lose it to a broken line. Taking turns, they both handled the rod throughout the next forty minutes, as I showed them how to let the fish run, wait until it was tired, then reel it back in until it ran again.

Slowly the runs became shorter and briefer until our catch was entering the treeline and the shallows. Then I took over, bringing in the last few feet with the rod in the left hand, handling the net with the right.

"There it is!" they yelled in unison as the first flash of silver and green rolled in the shady water. When it came ashore in the net, it was a big fat tench. Both youngsters were jumping up and down with excitement, Shane insisting on patting the catch, to be outraged on discovering it was covered in an oily slime.

The hook was easily slipped out of the lip when the pliers had snipped off the barb. I popped the tench in a sling and held up the weigh-scales. The arrow on the circular disc stopped at five pounds. Not a bad tench.

"Five pounds - wow," said Stuart as if he had caught tench all his life.

"Yeh. Wow," echoed Shane.

We admired it for a few seconds, lying panting on its side among the leaves, gave it a name (when you are three and five, everything must have a name) and then Thomas Tench was eased back into the water. He recovered fast, sniffed for the deeper water, flicked his tail and was gone.

On the way back to the car every other fisherman was approached to be told:

"We got a five pound tench."

Anglers are a kindly lot, and each one said:

"Well done lads, that's a good fish."

They were bursting with pride over that fish for days afterwards. Telling the postman, milkman, gardener and kindergarten teacher of their conquest in great detail.

That was eleven years ago. They are sixteen and fourteen now. Since then we have hunted the marlin and tuna off Mauritius where the great green swells of the Indian Ocean roll towards the reef. We have hauled monsters out of Halibut Hole at Glacier Bay, Alaska, and taken sailfish and shark from the Caribbean between Grenada in the south and north to the Florida Keys.

We have strained with cracking muscles against the mighty amberjack over the Four-Oh-Nine off Islamorada and stalked the tireless tarpon between the islands of Florida Bay. We have seen the yellowfin running in hundreds beneath the transom a hundred miles out in the Gulfstream of Port Canaveral.

With tanks on our backs we have watched the millions of creatures great and small that live beneath the water, while diving the North Wall of Grand Cayman and the grottoes of the British Virgins . . . . . But when I think of all the things we have seen and done together, of all the great fish we have taken and freed, and sometimes lost off the line, my thoughts always stray back to that summery day by the Cut Mill Pond at Elstead when we caught our first together - Thomas, the Five Pound Tench.

An Extract From 'Scouse Mouse'

By George Melly

In 1935, for the first time Tom and Gampa took me
fishing, something I'd begged them to do every year.
We drove down a little lane one fine afternoon and
Kane had to stop the car when a mother duck and about
six babies in her wake emerged from the grass and
waddled processionally across. We got to the fishing
hut by the River Clwyd and Tom and Gampa put up
three rods. They tied on flies for themselves and a big
worm for me. I sat on the bank watching my float and
listening to them bickering as they fished. Tom was
the more impatient. He cast all the time. Gampa
reproached him.

"What's the point of flogging the water, Tom? Wait
for a rise."

I found it quite funny but a bit disorientating to
hear my father told off like a small boy. Then my float
bobbed. I did nothing. I knew from catching perch at
Coniston that you didn't strike until it went under. It
was most likely to be an eel. Gampa said I'd probably
catch only eels. The float bobbed again a few times
and then moved steadily down towards the bottom. I
struck and gave an excited yelp as the rod bent double
and the line came screaming off the reel. Tom and
Gampa, shouting advice, ran towards me along the
bank.

Twenty minutes later my first trout, three pounds
in weight, lay on the grass in all its speckled glory. How
responsible was I for landing it? Very little I should

think, but they never took the rod off me. I believe my father stood behind me, his hands over mine, guiding them as to when to reel in, when to hold, when to let the fish run. Gampa netted it. When we got back to Hafod, Gampa wrote down in his fishing book:

DATE:	*Aug.15 1935*	**RIVER:**	*Clwyd*
FISH:	*Brown Trout*	**FLY:**	*Worm*
WEIGHT:	*3lb*	**REMARKS:**	*G.M.'s first trout*

After that Tom taught me to fly-fish, but I didn't have much success to begin with. The year we took Lount, there was a little stream at the bottom of the gnome-ridden garden. I was convinced there were trout in it, and cast away there hour after hour. One day Tom told me he thought the trouble was there were too many leaves and too much rubbish floating down the stream. He bought wire netting and some posts and we spent a morning erecting a barrier across it, both at the top end and more mysteriously, at the bottom. Two days later I hooked and landed a trout unaided. It was only six inches long but I had done it all by myself and insisted on having a photograph taken. It came out rather blurred, but you can just see the trout. I am holding it up by the tail, the rod in my other hand, and looking very proud and solemn. What Tom didn't tell me for ages was that there were no trout in that stream. He'd gone out one evening to a trout farm and bought half a dozen. The wire netting barriers had nothing to do with either leaves or rubbish. They were to prevent the trout he'd bought from swimming away.

The Fishing Competition

By Sophia Hills

In the year of 1990 me and my family went to Sweden for two weeks holiday. We stayed in my dad's flat that overlooked a small primary school and a park. One day when we were shopping in the town we met dad's boss - my dad worked in Sweden - he said,

"Come over to my place and meet my wife."

So after we had done the shopping, we set off to walk up the narrow, yellow path that went under the nearest motorway that went to Oslo. The path linked the housing estate for the town. We saw children playing hide and seek under ancient willow trees bending like old men with bad backs. Halfway towards our flat I saw my friend Renee playing in a small park. I shouted out,

"Hej Renee!" which means 'Hello Renee'.

As we walked past Renee spoke in Swedish to my dad. He translated what she had told him.

"There is a fishing contest on the river."

An hour later my dad got us down on the river with fishing lines dangling in the water. Something started to pull at the other end, I pulled my line out of the water and there it was, a long slimy fish with strands of flashing colour. Its mouth was open, as though someone had turned it to stone. I put it in the bucket. I picked up a maggot with my eyes shut, I didn't like it and put it back. My dad had to put it on the end of the line for me. I lowered the line into the river and waited until again I felt something pulling and the miniature buoy bobbed up and down. I reeled up my line and there was a little fish on the end. After that my brother and I fished for about an hour - then the results. As my dad worked in Sweden we fished for his company, Volvo. We did not win, but I enjoyed it.

In The Beginning

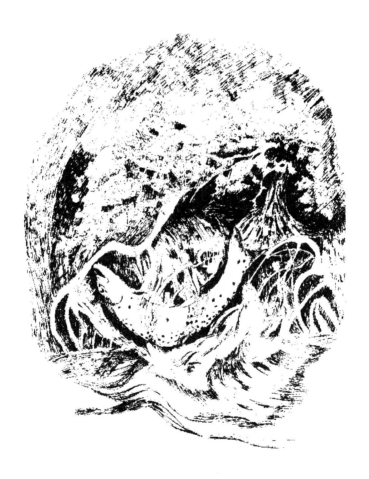

By Pat O'Reilly

In a little white house on the outskirts of Baltinglass, County Wicklow, the day was drawing to a close. The winter wood had been gathered in, the chickens fed, and Jimmy and I had gathered up the little bottles of oil, spare casts and the beautiful flies which I had spent all afternoon preening and admiring. No coat of many pockets for this young duo - me edging uncertainly into my teens and my mentor with all the worldly wisdom of a first year apprentice carpenter. Jimmy had been born beside the River Slaney and lived next door to George "The Doc" Abbot who was, we both knew, the greatest fisherman in all Ireland.

"The Doc" was a legendary figure even in those days. It was said that he spent most of his waking hours (and other people's sleeping hours) studying the river and its insect and fish life; rumour had it that he knew every trout over a pound by its unique pattern of spots. A likely tale too!

A tiny winged dry fly wafted into gentle glides and quiet pools was Jimmy's metier. I was relegated to raking the runs and searching the stickles with a wet Brown Rail and later when my line fell more often on water than on willow, with a team of two or three wet flies. I would fish until all my casts were impossible tangles, and then watch the master, quizzing him with a barrage of seemingly simple but usually answerable "whys" of rivercraft. I learnt mainly from watching.

Jimmy would move slowly upstream peering into the glassy surface until he spotted a worthy quarry. Then his fly would be anointed with oil and tapped gently against the cork handle of the cane rod. Two false casts and the line would fold down onto the surface as softly as straw blown on the evening breeze. Not daring to move, I would hold my breath until a splash confirmed that the deception was indeed complete. A half pounder, its tail whipping the black surface to cream, would be quickly brought to hand, given no chance to dive for the sanctuary of the weed. Despite the heavy rod pressure very few fish got off, and those that were returned had little time to ponder their plight before they were free once again.

On the tyro's outfit, five ounce trout occasionally came in two or three at a time, fighting one another. It was fun at first, but I soon yearned to copy the master and fish the dry fly. I think I managed to rise a few fish, but I can't recall making contact with anything other than weed and willow.

Through that summer in the early 'fifties, and in others to follow, Jimmy Doyle taught me how to fish for trout - no mean feat that, for I had the concentration span of a newly hatched sedge fly and about as much co-ordination. I was shown how to find the lies of the plumpest trout, how to stalk fish using every bit of cover and how to control the fly line in the air so that it fell on the surface without startling the fish. For the river fisher, this, I learned, was far more important than distance casting. And all this from a teenage tutor, long before fancy sounding qualifications were thought of.

The Upper Slaney, as I remember it, was a gentle river whose waters ran over limestone and produced great beds of water crowfoot with extra tough stems to withstand the winter spates. If you hooked the weed, often the only way to recover your fly was to get in the water; no great torture in those glorious summers of old. Except after a summer spate, Slaney trout were free risers, but I had no idea what they were taking. They came three to the pound the way I fished then, but Jimmy was always able to winkle out some bigger fish, a few of which we took home for breakfast: delicious!

And of course, the fishing was free.

In the forty years between then and now I had fished dozens of Irish rivers, yet somehow I hadn't got round to re-visiting the Slaney. But in the May of 1992 my wife and I finally made the pilgrimage. Leaving the ferry at Rosslaire we travelled up the Slaney past the Doyle fishery, famous for its spring salmon, through Tullow and Rathvilly until we topped a rise and looked down upon the little town of Baltinglass, gift-wrapped in emerald green and tied with silver ribbon. The ribbon shimmered in the midday sun as it wound its way via a weir at the north, down through the town and out again by Parkmill to the south. From half a meadow's distance we could see the tell-tale rings of rising trout, but first we needed fishing permits.

We tried the hardware shop, the chemist, the newsagent - all with the same response; a smile, a shrug, and, "Sure, I think you can just go and fish."

However, the newsagent did suggest that if we were at all worried we could ask the Garda.

The Garda officer smiled, shrugged and said,

"Sure, I think you can just go and fish."

And so it is on much of the upper river; a refreshing scarcity of "Fishing Preserved" signs. Further downstream, angling associations at Rathvilly and Tullow have some very attractive waters, and day tickets are available at little cost.

We started above the town on broad shallows with the occasional deep hole beneath the alders. There were tiddlers by the thousand rising to every speck that touched the surface. The bigger trout, mostly around five to six ounces were congregating in shoals wherever there was depth and shade. The fly on the water was the small dark olive for which a size 16 Greenwell's Glory, although on the big side, was a close enough imitation. The fish were easily spooked in the clear slow-flowing water, but a slight breeze rippled the surface and helped to conceal my leader. In two hours I covered just 250 yards, catching sixteen green-flanked trout with the brightest of crimson spots. When released, most of them swam straight back to their feeding lies none the worse for the experience, but perhaps a little wiser.

Later in the afternoon we moved downstream to where chestnuts shade the river and great beds of water crowfoot speed the surface current. Here the fish were less plentiful but bigger - averaging half a pound. Mayflies were hatching, and I was ready for that. On many Irish rivers the hatch can be too dense, making the chance of a trout taking your artificial almost nil. The Slaney isn't like that. The duns come off in good enough numbers to excite the trout while still leaving plenty of surface to cast at.

I put on a hackled mayfly and waded carefully up the edge of the river. Chest waders would have been ideal; I filled my thigh waders three times before deciding it wasn't worth stopping to empty them again. A good neb showed between two wracks of weed. It appeared again, and I waited half a minute before casting. There was no wind, the range was barely twelve yards, and my fly alighted perfectly just where I wanted it. I was alone in wanting it there. Again and again I tried, but with no response. Yet the trout continued to rise spasmodically, splashing in a way that told me he couldn't possibly be taking nymphs. There was only one possible answer; there must be some other fly on the water.

There was. In the shade of the trees, the surface appeared almost black - so dark that I hadn't noticed the black gnats drifting past. I had seen swarms of Bibio circling an inch above the water beneath the alders, but hadn't expected many to end up on the surface. By moving to where the river reflected the sky rather than the trees, I was able to see just how plentiful these little black casualties were.

On went a size 18 bi-visible black gnat and, first cast, it was accepted by the fussy feeder, a plump half pounder. More than a dozen of his tribe fell to the same fly in the next hour. "You would be proud of me Jimmy," I thought smugly. Then it was off to Parkmill to finish the evening rise on the waters of my fly-fishing baptism. This had been but a prelude, a warm up for the main event.

Nothing had changed except the gusting wind, which now blew downstream with a "have an early night" chill. If anything the trout were bigger than I remembered, although we met two other anglers - not many considering we covered four or five miles of river in two days - and both told us that the fishing had been even better a few years ago.

Déjà Vu

As we were tackling up, we saw two young lads climb the stile and set off across the meadow to fish the evening rise. The taller, and clearly the elder, was talking earnestly ; the younger nodding appreciatively. It may have been the evening breeze that misted my eye, but I had more than the usual difficulty seeing to tie on my fly.

On a fast bend beneath a willow I found a steady riser. He came first cast to a sedge, fought like a demon demented and finally buried his head in a weed-bed close to my bank. A cock fish nudging the pound mark, I marvelled at the speed with which he water-skied back to his bolt hole. Presumably when in a hurry he found it easier to take the surface route and so avoid the weed.

As I worked steadily upstream beside a high wire fence, I became aware of a pair of piercing eyes watching my every move. I nodded in acknowledgement and made a high steeple cast to cheat the gusting wind.

"It'll be the little black gnats they're after," came a voice from behind the wire.

"Thanks! I thought so. I'm fishing a size sixteen."

"An eighteen would be better," came the reply.

With no chance of seeing to change a fly now, and my torch back in the car, I nodded and worked my way up to a splashy riser beneath an alder on my bank.

"Watch your footing there, lad. There's a nasty hole in front of -"

"OK - Found it," I called gratefully. My watcher certainly knew the river.

The wind relented for a moment, and I was able to place my fly a few inches from where I judged the trout was lying. Up he came - a good splosh of a rise - and I had him, skipping across the surface, thrashing his tail angrily. A frisky half pounder skittered towards me, and I slid my fingers down the tapered leader to ease out the barbless hook - no need; this trout was a survival expert. The fish cartwheeled away towards freedom, still skipping on the surface as it surged upstream towards its alder root bolt hole. I turned to the fence expecting to hear "Bad luck" , but no. . . .

"Well done, lad," the old man said. "Well, I'll be getting along."

"Thanks," the middle aged lad replied. "And. . . goodnight, Doc.''

Food For Thought

By Peter Stone

Living a few hundred yards from the River Thames I was destined to become an angler. In winter my father went pike fishing while I sat impatiently at the window waiting for his return. Invariably his bag contained a pike which graced the dinner table the following day. Due to my lack of years I was not allowed to accompany my father and many tears were shed as he set off for his afternoon's enjoyment.

Those pike were the spark that ignited my desire to become an angler.

Although my father was a keen angler, he was not a good one and in truth, I learnt little from him. But he was an influence, always encouraging his mad-keen son and accompanying me whenever he could.

When I was seven, father took me to the local tackle shop and handed over 7/6d for a three jointed "general" rod. The two bottom joints were made from Tonkin cane, the top joint lancewood which, after I landed a few reasonable size fish, took a bad set. For many years the rod was my constant companion. Its victims included countless numbers of barbel, in which I specialised; chub, pike, roach, tench and eels. It was indeed a "general" rod. Finally, at the beginning of my teens, it was replaced by a much better rod. Now, minus the lancewood top, it resides in my tackle cupboard as a constant reminder of those happy and informative years.

During the Second World War I acquired a "class" reel made of bakelite with steel fittings. It came to me in a rather unusual way. My fishing companion at the time, Fred Smith, worked at the Cowley car works and one day several sackfuls of centre-pin reels arrived for melting down for steel. Fred smuggled two out and for many years that reel gave faithful service landing many fish, including some big ones. The reel now keeps the rod company in my cupboard.

Most of my fishing was done on the River Thames within a stone's throw of my home. Barbel were my main quarry, many of which I caught by trotting minnows in and around the weirpools. My setup was simple: 6lb breaking strain line (during the war years the line was thick sewing thread), a number 6 hook tied to gut, and a float made from a medicine bottle cork. The cork was cut in half and bored through the centre. The line was passed through the cork and secured in place by a piece of stick. The minnows, fished both dead and alive, were lip-hooked and the float set some three feet up the line. Two swan shot were pinched on the line one foot below the float.

The minnow was cast into a likely looking swim and allowed to travel downstream with the current. Bites were signalled by the float either travelling downstream faster than the flow (when the fish was swimming back downstream but remaining at the same depth) or simply disappearing. The strike was instantaneous and I rarely missed.

Initially I was puzzled by the latter bite. Later I discovered what caused the float to disappear so quickly. I was fishing the open river when I spotted several barbel lying some two feet below the surface. Setting the float 18 inches from the minnow I watched intently as the bait approached the quarry. Suddenly one turned over on its back, then righted itself. As it did so the float shot under. The barbel of course was forced to turn over to take the minnow due to its underslung mouth.

Readers may wonder why I preferred a piece of cork to a proper float. When advising youngsters, I emphasize the importance of keeping things simple and as natural as possible. The majority of my barbel were taken in shallow water and I wondered whether a painted float passing overhead might scare them. It may, it may not, but when in doubt - don't. A piece of cork however, with a stick pushed through it, looked nothing more than a piece of rubbish. Fish see plenty of that floating over their heads.

Remember also that fish - especially big ones - often live in places in to which it is difficult to cast a bait. But never worry about that; if you think fish are present then find a way of getting your bait to them. Never worry about getting a fish out; the hardest part is getting it ON. Achieve that THEN start worrying.

During my schooldays my village was inhabited by several characters, one of them, a farmer, took exception to me. He owned a field through which a three foot deep ditch, inhabited by hundreds of small chub, dace and roach, flowed. During the winter the ditch provided my supply of livebaits for pike fishing. One morning I was catching these livebaits when I heard a shout.

"Oi you. Out!"

The farmer was leaning against the gate a hundred yards away. Sheepishly I obeyed his command but took care to leave the bait bucket behind.

"Don't let me see you in here again," he growled as I walked past.

Stopping a short distance away, I waited until he cycled off; then I returned to the ditch. Twenty minutes and several livebaits later I heard him shout again and for the second time I picked up my tackle, but not the bait can, and left.

"I told you not to come back do you hear? Keep out and stay out."

"Yes sir," I muttered.

This time I walked further on to the main river and started fishing. Half an hour later the farmer cycled past towards the village. Ten minutes later I was catching more livebait. But I suspected that he might return. An hour later I looked round; he was leaning on the gate staring in my direction. But he said nothing and I fished on until I had sufficient for my needs. By then he had departed. Strangely he never turned me out again. What a cheeky little so and so I was.

One of my favourite haunts was a backwater of the Thames. Fifteen yards wide, the gin-clear water flowed through dense patches of rananculus where occasionally, brown trout leapt clear of the water. Here, dozens of pike were caught, destined for our family dinner plate. Scores of barbel including many over eight pounds fell to trotted minnows and ledgered cheesepaste. On one unforgettable morning a four pound chub - my first ever "four" - took a liking to my ledgered breadcrust.

Today, the backwater is half its previous width; the rananculus and the barbel have long since disappeared; the trout long before that.

But the saddest sight of all is the ditch. Today, completely devoid of water, it is just a depression in the field, the result of abstraction and "improvements" to the river by man. I still pass it regularly. Then I stop and cast my mind back to the hours spent catching livebait from the once clear water; the farmer leaning on the gate watching my every, well almost every, move. Wonderful days, days during which I learnt so much about the river and its inhabitants.

The Great Big Fish

By Grant Wallis

One Saturday afternoon at exactly 2pm I went fishing over the back of Bromley Bowling Club. I set up my rod and all my fishing gear and sat down.

I cast my line into the lake and then all of a sudden I felt something pull at the other end. Then I tried to pull it in to land on the grass but I couldn't manage it. The thing on the other end of the line tugged on the rod again. This time I fell into the water. Suddenly I was getting dragged along by an enormous (well I thought it was) an enormous fish. It dragged me through the water like the fish was a speedboat and I was the person hanging on. The fish seemed to get faster and faster as it went along.

Suddenly it turned round and was heading straight for the shore. At the edge of the water it stopped dead and I was sent flying over the fish's back and landed head first in a bush.

Someone came out of the bowling club, saw me and called the fire brigade to come and get me down. After about an hour they came to save me. They did but it was a bit embarrassing when I split my trousers open and people could see my boxer shorts.

After that I went back to see if I could find the big fish. I saw it laying on the grass ready for me to take home to eat with my family.

I couldn't believe it.

A Day To Remember

By John Goddard

It was a lovely bright summer day when just after lunch I collected my eight year old grandson, Christopher, for his first ever day's fishing. Looking back, I well remember my first day's fishing at about the same age, when my father took me to a local pond for my first experience of this wonderful sport. We went complete with twopenny net and a jam jar which was soon to be filled with neat looking little sticklebacks that absolutely fascinated me at the time.

Today would be a little different as the equipment I had brought for Christopher was far more sophisticated and in keeping with this modern age in which we live now. A modern fixed-spool reel, a supple and springy 14ft float rod, rod rest, keepnet and even a couple of comfortable chairs for us to sit upon, plus of course, a pint of wriggling maggots and enough groundbait to fill a bucket. Nothing had been spared to make his first outing a success.

The venue that I had chosen was a lovely little tree-lined local pond that I had been assured held some very nice fish. On one side of the pond were private dwellings and I had obtained permission from a friend who lived there to fish from the bottom of his garden. Upon our arrival our first task was to set up the tackle followed by a brief lesson on how to hold the rod and strike. Next, how to pump the rod when and if a fish took the bait as I felt it important that he should be given every opportunity to hook and play his first fish on his own. The setting was perfect and with no wind the polished tranquil surface of the pond reflected the many trees against the opposite bank, absolutely superb for float fishing.

Mixing a liberal supply of groundbait I proceeded to bait the swim and mount three juicy maggots on the hook five feet below the float. Despite his best efforts Christopher found it impossible to cast the float out into the swim. To be fair, the rod was really too big for him and a high bank behind us did not help; in the end I was forced to take over this part of the operation. We sat side by side on the two chairs waiting for the action. I explained that it was vital to watch the float like a hawk for any sign of movement and then as soon as it slipped below the surface to strike. After half an hour nothing had happened and I could sense that he was becoming a little restless. I managed to re-kindle his interest by recounting some fishing experiences. At the end of the first hour the float had not even trembled and it looked as if set in molten lead. By now even I was becoming a little disillusioned and beginning to have serious doubts as to whether there were in fact any fish in this pond.

Throwing in some more groundbait I tried to arouse Christopher's growing lack of interest. I knew that I was starting to lose the battle when he suddenly said, "Grandad I'm bored."

By now it was very hot and with the sun blazing down out of a clear blue sky; I must have dozed off. When I came to a little while later the chair beside me was empty. Looking around, I observed my grandson in the middle of the lawn swinging his arms.

"What on earth are you doing?" I asked.

Back came the obvious answer, "I'm practising my golf swing grandad."

He had recently been having golf lessons. With some difficulty I persuaded him to return to his seat and explained the need for patience when fishing.

After an hour and a half I was wondering what else I could do to tempt the apparently non-existent fish when I thought I saw a slight ripple round the float. I told Christopher to pick up the rod quickly as I thought we had a bite. After a few more seconds the float began to bob up and down. As it began to slide away from us and disappear beneath the surface I said, "Strike!"

This he did in fine style but unfortunately for me he struck sideways nearly taking my head off and catapulting me over the back of the chair and straight into a puddle of muddy water. By the time I had recovered the fish had taken quite a bit of line and Christopher was hanging on like grim death. Easing the clutch off a little I told him to pump and wind just as I had shown him. To his credit, he accomplished this extremely well.

Within the next few minutes, which felt like hours, he struggled until the fish suddenly seemed to give up and surfaced under the rod tip. At this juncture, I had to give him some help to land the fish as there was a band of weed growing out from the bank over which we had to land it. Sliding the landing net under the fish, I eased it onto the bank where I saw that it was the most lovely tench of well over two pounds. It was really handsome with bottle green flanks and bright red eyes. I shall long remember this moment and Christopher's look of pure joy as he slid the fish into the keepnet. What a marvellous fish to catch on his first ever fishing expedition. I recall that it was fifteen years before I caught my first tench and even then it was smaller than this one.

Throwing in some more groundbait to keep the fish interested we had to wait less than ten minutes for the next bite. On this occasion Christopher was too eager and pulled the bait out of the fish's mouth. Not so with the next bite which came shortly after. I think more by luck than judgement he timed his strike perfectly just as the float disappeared below the surface. This time the fish took a lot of line and started circling in deeper water, so I had to give Christopher some rapid instruction.

"Lift the rod tip high and point it to the sky, then lower it and wind like mad."

He thought this was great and kept repeating it after me as he worked on the fish. Eventually he had the still unseen fish circling deep down under the rod tip and I had to give him a hand to get it to the surface. I scooped up what appeared to be a shining bar of gold into the landing net. Carrying the fish onto the lawn, I laid it on the turf where Chris was so excited he could hardly gasp out, "Look, Grandad its got red fins."

The body was the deepest gold and with its bright red fins it really was a spectacular looking fish. This was a rudd of well over two and a half pounds and a much rarer fish than the tench. I remember thinking that it was really turning out to be a day to remember. Showing Christopher how to gently remove the hook before sliding the great fish into the keepnet to join the tench, he could barely wait to get back to the water's edge to continue fishing.

At this point, while I hoped that he would catch some more fish, I secretly wished that they would be small ones; I did not want Christopher to get the impression that a day's fishing would always be like this. However, it was not to be. Over the next two hours he caught four more super fish. Two of them were beautiful rudd over two pounds and one somewhat smaller together with another tench close to two pounds. Even for me this would have been an outstanding day, but for an eight year old this must have been really exceptional. I can only hope that if he takes up fishing seriously he will not be put off by the inevitable blank days when only the very small fish seem to be biting.

Arriving home later that afternoon my wife said to him, "Well, did you catch anything Christopher?"

His answer must be one of the greatest understatements of all time.

"But of course Nana. We've been fishing."

That was two years ago; since then I have only taken him fishing on a couple of occasions, on one of which he landed a bream of over five pounds. He is now involved in so many sports at school that he has little time for such a mundane pastime as fishing. I have started giving him casting lessons with a fly rod and when he is sufficiently proficient will introduce him to the love of my life, fly-fishing for trout.

A Conversation With . . .

. . . Guess Who?

The boy grew up in post-war Shepherds Bush, London. It was an area rich in community even if not well endowed financially. The numerous bomb sites that remained unclaimed for what seemed like many years were also rich.

"All the bomb sites were like huge wildlife reserves. They built bloody council estates on them and gradually took away our playgrounds."

He treasured these havens and a desire to live in the country was thus instilled in him from an early age. It was not long before the boy was drawn to water. At the age of ten he was heading north to Willesden and Old Oak Common, trudging through the streets to his chosen venue. The Grand Union Canal threaded its dusty filmed way beside the vast railway yards. These magic places provided additional interest on the way there or back.

So to the serious business. A bicycle wheel rim, a sack and a length of string were scavenged from the surrounding debris. These unlikely components were assembled in a somewhat Heath Robinson manner. The result was a piece of angling equipment guaranteed to bring home the catch. The quarry? What could survive in such lifeless waters? What did every boy fish for? The hardy stickleback of course.

With the sack draped seductively from the rim, the trap was lowered into the murky water. As the innocent fish swam over the familiar bicycle part below, a quick lift and . . . captured. So easy.

He was a youth of 15 before the next major advance in his angling education came about. Expelled from school on his 15th birthday, he took an apprenticeship as a sheet metal worker and could afford proper fishing tackle. He decided to stick with the tried and tested materials; he invested in an aluminium "Taperflash" rod.

Travelling west this time, he found himself on the banks of the Potomac Pond in Gunnersbury Park, Acton. This small lake of some three acres, surrounded by railings, nestled in a corner of the park. Traffic on the forerunner of the M4 was just a distant rumble in those days.

Although small, this was a classic parkland water. Deep and dark with an island in one corner; a liberal covering of lily pads and plenty of trees with their roots testing the water. To add an air of mystery, a folly in the form of a tower loomed over one bank. The place had a certain air of seclusion.

It was obviously full of fish. Indeed the youth did make contact with one, albeit only briefly.

His float slid beneath the surface.

"I hadn't quite got the hang of striking."

The two inch roach emerged like a Polaris from the depths. It was prevented from going into orbit by an overhanging tree. The unfortunate fish spent its final moments there fluttering in the breeze like a silver leaf.

"I felt extremely sorry for the poor thing and I apologised profusely to it."

This minor achievement gave him hope that his keepnet would soon be bulging . . . it eventually dawned on him that perhaps this was not to be. His mentor, Clive Bowey, was catching them all. He spent the rest of the day meditating.

"I took a liking to it. Just sitting by the water pretending to be doing something."

His yearning for the country stayed with him. Even in those early days he would dream of his very own private fishery.

Our hero was also a member of a rock band. Nights spent playing two noisy, sweaty, smokey sessions until perhaps four in the morning were often followed by a couple of hours fishing.

"It was the perfect antidote to a heavy night's clubbing. It really levelled you out."

He was now heading further west. Gravel pits between West Drayton and Sunbury where fabulous free fishing for perch could be found.

"No one ever bothered us. There were never any signs up."

But all good things must come to an end. After six months of peace the sky darkened as a cloud in the form of a "jobsworth" drifted across the sun.

"You got a ticket mate?"

And so another haven of tranquillity was no longer available.

Still further west he travelled, to Langley and his old friend the Grand Union. A cleaner stretch this time with tench as the quarry. More hectic nights of rock. A drive to the waterside, a couple of hours fishing. . . . then sleep.

Time moved on. Worldwide success for the band. With success came money and the opportunity to travel even further west. Halfway round the world this time for big game fishing in The Florida keys. He felt elated when he caught his first sailfish.

"I had it mounted like everybody does. I fell for that one."

Eventually, revulsion took over when he realised that these giants of the ocean were being fed to the sharks after capture.

At last, the subject of this story realised the childhood dream spawned beside the Grand Union Canal and the Potomac Pond. From a stream that trickled through his farm he created a secluded fishery where he discovered his ultimate angling experience - fly-fishing for trout. These days, many anglers are able to enjoy the peaceful surroundings of Lakedown. They too can unwind in deepest Sussex.

The owner, Roger Daltrey, says of fishing:

"It takes the stress out of life. The amount of good it does is unresearched. Much better than a Mogadon."

Even with all his experiences Roger can cast his mind back to his childhood.

"I still get pleasure sitting with my son down by the carp lake. There's something about being by water. Just being there for a few hours seems to unload all your troubles."

Quality Time

By Steve Windsor

I did not have the childhood privileges my children enjoy. For, perfect though my childhood was, I was a suburban North Londoner.

I hope my children will enjoy the privileged adulthood I am enjoying with a good job with a secure nationally successful company far from the cares of commuting and big city life. But for now, they can join me in the quiet drive to a little trout stream which curves from village to village on the Lincolnshire/ Leicestershire borders. It's what the Americans call quality time.

Quality for me, as I flick flies down the little jump-across brook, and catch wild browns of a few ounces which end up in my son's tiddler net, and the occasional solid stock fish.

Quality time for Hannah and Magnus, as they flit from the fishing and the fauna to a child's version of beachcombing (riverbank raking) where sheep's wool, pieces of stone, twigs and a few wild flowering weeds rapidly fill my pockets.

We talk about everything, from life and the meaning of the universe, to whether its possible to have brushed your teeth and have a dry toothbrush . . .

I miss a lot of fish, scare a lot more, walk miles with the constant request to return to "see the little lambs" ringing in my ears, and generally chase away the cares of the day, and prepare little heads for the pillow. My concentration is non-existent, and there's no question that I catch more when I venture forth alone.

I don't care about the arguments one way or the other. The little wild brownies are too beautiful not to go back into the water; the big stockies are bred to be used in what is often a chancey form of pick your own and to end up on the table. But most of these go back too, so that my fellow members can have their rods bent by a better fish. I live in hope that I'll continue to contact these better fish through the year. But one-by-one their numbers are thinned, and by late June it's mostly wild fish that provide the sport.

As good Anglo-Finns my children understand that food swims in the seas and rivers, that it must be killed to be eaten, and that it has blood and guts that must be removed. They accept this, and have eaten what they've caught themselves.

But what is nice is the balance they have already achieved. The first good fish of the season was taken home to show mummy, and duly eaten. That done, there was no need to show their surrogate success - the pleasure with future fish was to carefully slip them back.

There's only one real problem with our riverside rambles. It really isn't an easy place to fish, lined with trees and jungles of grass. It's no place to teach a child to cast, and despite the rules that allow me to share a rod with them, and their frequent requests, the art will have to be learnt elsewhere before it can be applied here.

And if it's never learnt, and in ten years time they look upon fly-fishing as Dad's little eccentricity, it won't be a problem. We will still have those spring and summer nights of cuckoo, cowslip, flies and fleece, and those long walks through the dew wet crops as we return to the car. Beats the hell out of the Grand Union Canal at Greenford.

The Seeds Are Sown

By Bob Carnill

I have always maintained that a true fisherman is born
- as opposed to being a product of circumstance - due,
perhaps, to he or she having inherited more than an
average amount of prehistoric "hunter'" genes. Having
said that; it doesn't mean to say that anyone who has a
mind to fish, shouldn't totally enjoy the experience.

On reflection, from a very early age, I exhibited all
the signs symptoms and emotions of a born fisherman.
My earliest recollection of this phenomenon, is of me
standing over a bucket of water that contained my
father's livebait for the morrow's pike fishing
expedition. Being about four years old at the time, I
wouldn't be included on the trip - but my intense
concentration and fascination as I stood peering down
into that bucket, etched an indelible image of those
half dozen small roach deep into my memory. As they
hung almost motionless in the water near the bottom,
everything about them excited me; the slightest
movement of a fin, the opening and closing of the gill
covers, the tiniest eye movement, and the pattern of
the scales are as vivid now - 50 years on - as they were
then.

However, within the year I was to embark on the
greatest adventure of my life: Dad had rigged a small
saddle and a pair of stirrups to the crossbar of his ancient
black pedal cycle - and I was going fishing with HIM.

The big day eventually arrived and we left our tiny
terraced house in the St Ann's district of Nottingham;

cycling first along the St Ann's valley and into the city centre, and then down into the meadows - another district of terraced houses, home to miners and industrial workers and their families, beyond which lay the River Trent and exciting green fields. This was indeed a great adventure. It was from this locality - after graduating through a series of "easier" fish: struts (minnows), whitling (bleak), and gudgeon that I finally caught my very first and long awaited trophy; a six ounce silver-sided roach with red-tinged fins - just like those in the bait bucket that had first fired my imagination not that many months earlier.

For several years - until I grew too big for the crossbar seat - Dad continued to take me fishing on the cycle, during which time he coached me in the art of long-trotting, laying-on and ledgering. However, in between times a firm partnership had been struck up between Dad and two St Ann's businessmen; Harry Bramley the butcher and Charlie Halliday the gent's hairdresser. In those far off days not many people owned a car - in fact it was a status symbol if you knew somebody who did own a car! None-the-less, Charlie had one, and each Sunday morning he would pick Dad and I up before setting off to Harry's house.

Looking back, I can't help but compare them to those three heroes in the "Last of the Summer Wine" - albeit a much younger version. Each was as different as chalk and cheese, and each was a real character in his own right. Dad was the spitting image of Arthur Askey; small, full of fun and wit, and as active as a Jack Russell. Charlie, on the other hand, was tall, slim, angular in face and body, and hobbled around on terribly bunioned feet. Harry was a James Mason look-alike and as eccentric as they come.

Everything about Harry was measured and calculated - he was as reliable as night following day. Even in the mid '40s, Harry stood out in a crowd; a straw boater, plus-fours, open-toe sandals, waistcoat, tweed jacket and dicky-bow was his daily attire - even on our Sunday fishing trips!

Dad and I always sat in the back seat, leaving the front passenger seat free for Harry, and even now I only have to close my eyes to re-live the ritual of arriving at Harry's. He would always be waiting outside; an imposing figure with the bare minimum of fishing tackle; a small bag and one rod. On opening the car door he would lean in and greet us with a thick lipped beaming smile and. . . ."Good morning gentlemen, I trust you are all well." After which he would light three cigarettes, hand them round - and then we would set off. I can still smell the freshly lit tobacco smoke on the fresh morning air, mixed, as it was, with sharper more acrid fumes of the match - and remember how I wished I was old enough to have a puff. Who says that children can't be influenced by the habits and actions of adults?

One of my favourite fishing venues in those days was
the Little Witham River out at Barnby-in-the-Willows
- a sleepy little village with a tiny and very ancient
church which sat almost on the banks of the stretch
we fished. Each and every Sunday morning the bells of
the church would peal out over the surrounding
countryside setting a scene of sheer tranquillity and
bliss. This really was my favourite place. The river ran
narrow and clear over a clean gravel bottom and
through verdant flowing weedbeds, thus providing rich
feed for the abundant shoals of huge roach, chub and
dace - which in turn maintained an ample head of pike;
a fish I was in awe of - and had yet to catch.

Hardly surprising then, that my very first pike came
from a deep, rush fringed pool just downstream of the
church. However, like all pike fishing venues, the Little
Witham was either famine or feast and on the day in
question it was the first time I had fished there when
the pike were "on" and oh boy were they "on". The
three adults fished the swim first, each in turn, and
each trotting a roach livebait down the stream, close
to the edge of the rushes; and every time the large pike
bung would be snatched below the surface accompanied
by a huge swirl which made my young heart leap and
my hands shake. The sheer size, speed and voracity of
the fish left me quaking and in a strange state - a feeling
of fear coupled with excitement.

It wasn't too long before three good pike lay on the bank - and it was my turn to take the rod. With more than a little trepidation, I stepped forward, tossed the livebait into the swim, and began hand-feeding the heavy line from a Nottingham centre-pin reel. Down and down it steadily floated, suspended some 18 inches below the brightly painted bung. The float was nearing the end of the bed of rushes where the river takes a left-hand turn. . . ."Why hadn't I had a take," I asked myself... "Have they finally gone off - or have they all been caught?"

The slamming of the bung beneath the surface jarred me back to reality, leaving me once again shaking from head to foot - and almost wishing the bait had never been taken.

"Don't strike, Bob," Dad's voice rang out... "Walk down the bank and reel in the slack line as you go."

This I did, and soon I could see the bung about a foot or so under the water and hanging motionless - the pike, unseen, was somewhere below it.

"Right, Bob, hold your reel tight and strike upwards," encouraged Dad. As the hooks went home, the pike shot off upstream like a rocket - with me running after it on wobbly legs.

I've always found river pike to be that much more athletic than their stillwater brethren; not only are they fitter, but they tend to use the current to their advantage; thus, this seven and a half pounder gave me quite a run around before finally slipping over the rim of the landing net. Once on the bank and dispatched - by one of the elders - I spent an age investigating every square inch of my prize. I was overjoyed, elated, and a little more at ease with the monster that previously frightened the life out of me.

Nowadays - and quite rightly so - the killing of such splendid sport fish is frowned upon; but back in the '40s with rationing still lingering on well after the war, a fat summer-fed pike was not something one slipped back into the water: it was looked upon as a welcome delicacy - not to mention its high protein content. Funnily enough, Mr Crabtree of Daily Mirror cartoon-strip fame, used to tell his son Peter . . . "There's scarcely a fish to beat a pike for flavour in sea or fresh water . . . and that a seven pound pike was a nice size for the table."

Mine was seven and a half pounds - perfect for Mum, a supercook of the old school.

That evening - after I had been given time to gloat over my first pike - Mum skinned and filleted the fish; the fillets were then put into brine to stand until the following day. There were no home fridges or freezers then; you used your food as it became available - or gave it away to friends and neighbours. Mum's method of cooking was simple, fast and delicious - as most good recipes are. The brined fillets were rinsed, drained, patted damp-dry between a tea towel, cut into portions, and finally rolled in seasoned flour. The fillets were then deep fried until their outer coat was crisp. They were served with thick-cut crispy potato chips - a meal fit for a king.

No More Fish

By Laura Patel

Swimming fish are nice to see,
Any fish is good for me.
Looks like fish for tea.
Mum says, "Feed your tum with cod."
On and on fish from God.
No more fish, please oh God, no more cod.

Call of The Sea

By Tony Gubba

My love of angling began at the age of ten when I went to live in Blackpool, on the west coast of Lancashire. Before then I'd only ever dangled for tiddlers in park lakes, but in the restless grey swell of the Irish Sea I discovered the joy and fascination of sea fishing.

The resort's famous Central Pier was only a ten minute walk from our front door, and twice a day when the tide was in, this finger of Victorian iron work became a small boy's magic carpet out to a wonderland beyond the funfairs and slot machine arcades occupied by the holidaymakers. At its beginning, nearest the promenade, the pier was wide and timber-floored, with a theatre, sideshows and candyfloss stalls. But at its end, extending further out to sea was a second, lower, level perhaps only six feet wide with an iron grating floor and a small unmanned light that flickered in the dark to warn shipping.

It was from here that we fished. With sturdy rods, heavy centre-pin reels and line strong enough to lasso a small liner, we would chuck the ornate metalwork of paternosters and spiked lead weights out into the sea and down, down to the sandy bottom twenty feet below. This was usually a three hook rig baited with lugworm and the rod left propped against the guardrail with a clothes peg bell clipped to the tip. If my eyes tired of watching for a knock I could always rely on the tinkling bell to attract my attention. It was wonderful fun and there was never a shortage of grateful recipients for the catch that might include dabs, whiting and cod.

When the sea was too rough and the pier was closed, I would take a tram ride up the promenade to the North Wall and cast off the paved walkway into the breaking waves. With a storm brewing up, the wind stinging exposed hands and face and a salty taste on the lips, it could be quite raw and a mite dangerous. I had to be alert to the occasional rogue wave that could drench me or, heaven forbid, wash me completely off the wall.

The discomforts of cold hands and chapped and chafed skin were of no consequence to an excited small boy; the fishing always seemed to be better when the sea was rough. I pictured myself as a lifeboat coxswain on a pitching deck protected by waterproofs and warm clothing. It was a journeyman's introduction to fishing, a working class baptism without the refinements of chalkstream fly-fishing for trout or the scenic splendour of a Scottish salmon river. Those delights would be discovered much later.

I suppose many thousands of youngsters like me have discovered the joys of fishing on an expedition to the end of the pier. I often wonder if kids still fish at weekends and evenings off the lower level of Central Pier. Are there any dabs and codling left to catch?

Yet even the thrill of landing a big dab or codling was surpassed when, a few years later, I was introduced to night lines. Around the coast of Britain there are many variations on the technique, but Blackpool in the fifties had its own method. We would attach a brick or plank of wood to each end of the line and then bury it in the sand as an anchor, keeping the whole line taut in one place. Hooks were tied on foot long droppers, spaced a couple of feet apart, with any number up to a hundred on one line. Digging the bait to arm such a contraption was often a day's work in itself.

The best combination of time and tide was when high water occurred around midnight. Then I could set the night line in early evening, as far out as possible on the exposed sands, to wait for the advancing tide to cover it before returning home to yearn for dawn. The 5am ringing of the alarm clock was rarely needed as I had usually been awake all night, too excited to sleep.

The streets were cold and deserted as I hurried out next morning to collect the harvest. It was always advisable to take a stout bag or box to bring home the catch. As the tide receded, I followed it out, looking for the tell-tale sign of a fish rolling in the surf that would show where the line was. It was unusual if nothing had been caught. Often, from those hundred hooks, I might retrieve a fine basket of half-a-dozen codling and perhaps a dozen dabs. It meant plenty of fish for tea.

Even now, four decades on, I still enjoy the memory of setting night lines on Blackpool sands and I'd love to do it again. OK, so it wasn't fishing in its truest sense. But whether I set night lines or cast off the end of the pier, it didn't really matter. That life-long love of angling was kindled in the soul.

The Pet Salmon

By Charles Parkes

Some boys will tell you that it is the excitement of sneaking a salmon from under the bailiff's nose, rather than financial gain, that motivates them. Consequently, the keen, astute bailiff and the furtive youths become engaged in a never ending battle of wits with victories for both sides.

Foxy was only thirteen but was fully experienced in the craft of taking salmon by any means possible - except by any legal method. He lived with his father in a cottage close to the Hampshire Avon. He sought his education in the fields and by the river as he spurned the confines of the classroom. He had learnt enough to fool the bailiffs if captured, always had the right answer - delivered in an annoyingly smug fashion.

Phil White, the bailiff, had earlier seen a light in Foxy's cottage; the door had opened to let the skinny, pointed silhouette of his arch enemy slither into the night carrying what appeared to be a bucket. The bucket aroused his curiosity. He had been a water bailiff for many years and thought he knew all of the poacher's illegal methods and tricks but a bucket had never been part of them. He had run over the fields and settled into a hideout of bramble and hawthorn some fifty yards from the Duke's Pool. Phil passed the time thinking of the many occasions he had just missed catching Foxy in the act. The times that they had exchanged greetings on the river bank when the boy had that "I know what I've been up to" glint in his eye. Perhaps this was to be Phil's day.

A rattling pebble on the stone strewn bank woke Phil from his daydream as the morning breeze rolled the mist away from the pool to reveal the unmistakable shape of Foxy's body, the bucket at his side. Resisting the temptation to run forward and grab him, Phil watched and listened hoping to get the evidence he needed. There was a splashing, ringing sound as if a fish was thrashing about in a half-filled bucket of water.

At last Phil had caught him with a live fish. He had come across Foxy several times with a dead one only to be met with such excuses as "I just found this one floating down the river Mr White. Looks diseased to me so I thought I would bring it back for you to examine." Or, "You've had poachers Mr White. I couldn't sleep so I went for a walk and found three of the blighters hiding this in the bushes. Is there a reward?"

Phil, unable to contain his excitement any longer, ran to Foxy's side: he appeared most unperturbed at being caught red-handed.

"Got you this time Foxy!" Phil proclaimed in a triumphant but rather breathless West Country brogue.

"Got me! How do you mean Mr White?" replied Foxy in his quizzical, cheeky way.

"Caught you with a live salmon, that's what I mean. It's the magistrate for you this time," crowed Phil.

"But this is my pet salmon. I can't be had up for a pet salmon," Foxy bleated indignantly.

He had lost cases before through some lame half-baked excuse concocted by the poacher. The thought of Foxy evading conviction sent a shiver through him as his moment of joyful revenge was momentarily arrested.

"Your pet salmon is it Foxy? You'll be laughed out of court with that one. Nobody has a salmon for a pet," retorted Phil, his air of confidence tinged with doubt.

"It's true Mr White," declared Foxy detecting the faintest possibility of a light at the end of an escape tunnel. "Isn't it Sammy?" he added for good measure and effect, looking to the floundering salmon in the bucket for confirmation.

Phil was dumbfounded. After all, he had seen him leave home with the bucket. It had to be one of Foxy's wiles. But what if it wasn't? Phil decided to play Foxy along for the time being.

"And what do you and your pet salmon do?"

"I keep Sammy in the bath and once a week I bring him down to the river for a swim. After about twenty minutes I give him a whistle and he comes back."

Foxy said this in a casual, matter-of-fact tone of voice. The light in the tunnel grew brighter.

"Can't you see that Sammy's all excited - he was just about to dive in when you came up," he added accusingly.

Phil roared with laughter. The more he laughed the more the doubt in his mind diminished. He picked up the gauntlet thrown down by this cheeky young whippersnapper.

"Let's see Sammy go for a swim then. Let's see you whistle him back," Phil challenged, thinking what a good yarn he would be able to spin at the next meeting of the fly-dressers guild.

Foxy lifted Sammy gently into the water and after a momentary pause to establish his bearings, Sammy gave a flick of his tail and glided into the river. Phil checked his watch. Foxy leaned back against an old tree trunk, his hands behind his head in a very nonchalant pose. Neither of them spoke throughout the twenty minutes, although Phil managed the occasional "Pet salmon indeed!" in a tense chuckle under his breath, whilst glancing riverward for a glimpse of an approaching fin.

"Time's up Foxy. Let's hear you whistle your salmon."

"Salmon Mr White? What salmon?"

A Guiding Hand

By Barrie Rickards

Childhood angling has always been seen by adults through a Hovis haze, sepia tinted, windless, and with a warm sun. The better catches and imagined skills are remembered: the problems forgotten. For these and other reasons adult instructors tend to expect too much skill too quickly. It takes months, not weeks, for an eight-year-old to become reasonably proficient at casting a 2BB float rig; and certainly it cannot be achieved in an afternoon's teaching, no matter how exalted is the teacher or enthusiastic the club. Children need very basic instructions and reasonable tackle, and then they need to be left alone to go fishing on a suitable water. Youngsters need to achieve on their own or they'll soon lose interest in the sport.

When this writer was a youth he inherited a set of tackle from his maternal grandmother: no-one else in the family fished, so the basic instruction was meted out by Bernard Venables in a little book called "Fish and Fishing", a Puffin book. I wonder if Bernard even remembers it! My copy was bought as a birthday gift by cousins, and I still have it; armed with this knowledge, second-hand, and my grandmother's tackle, I went a-fishing. For six months I didn't catch a thing. Not a fish. I tried various stillwaters in east Yorkshire before I discovered that my Racine tortue line was of 15lbs breaking strain and that a size 14 eyed hook to the end of it was no way to catch a fish. That's what I mean by saying that youngsters need a certain amount of basic instruction. I got mine from an old gent whom I befriended at Kiplin pond, near Hauden. I went back to look at the water before I wrote this piece, and a lady I presumed to be the new owner came out of the converted windmill and looked daggers at me. If her eyes had been loaded I'd be dead now. How sad. How times change! But even she cannot eclipse the memories.

That six months taught me something. For a start, youngsters do not need to catch fish to stay with fishing! A lot of adults make that mistake when teaching, and the object of a lot of instruction seems to be to get some fish on the kids' hooks, by any means possible, (including hooking them on for them, or handing them the rod when a fish has been hooked - again, starting is a skill that takes time). All this is wrong for MOST children. Far better would it be to take them fishing for a day, preferably on a one-to-one basis. Let them enjoy the day as a whole, and let fish take a secondary place. It does them no harm to see YOU catching: they'll recognise the skill needed then. GOING fishing then becomes as enjoyable as actually catching fish, and you have to go fishing to learn the skills, over a reasonable period - say a season.

Another important thing to remember is that children under ten years old have an attention span of no more than fifteen minutes. Even if they are pulling out fish every cast they will be distracted by the urge to climb trees or whatever. Let them. I remember my own son, aged six, catching one after another. When sixty were in the net, and the bites showing no signs of letting up, he simply "upped and off" for a bit of exploring. Plan your day in fifteen minute packages, such as fishing, food, explore, fishing, food, etc. and you'll hold their interest for a long time. They'll want to go fishing again.

Between the ages of ten and fifteen the attention span may rise to as much as two hours. Youngsters fishing completely on their own, as I did, may well stay out all day, nominally fishing, but in reality their day is spent as much wandering the banks as fishing. And, for sure, there'll be plenty of eating going on! It's important that young anglers can fish with those facilities. It's no good at all if they are on waters where they get slagged off for wandering the banks or climbing trees. Young anglers' waters are needed.

And now I'll relate one anomaly which ought to engage the minds of those club anglers designated to look after the young anglers in their ranks. It is this:

the attention span of the real youngsters when fishing is, as I have said, about fifteen minutes give or take a bit; the attention span of those same youngsters if involved in pond-dipping with a little net, is anything up to three hours! I have seen this many times. Now, think of the value of pond-dipping to would-be anglers. They'll learn all about the water life which is tied into the fish's world - invertebrates and plants. And they learn about the smaller fish species that are so crucial to the fishy pyramid of our waters, the loach and bullheads and sticklebacks. It does seem to me that our clubs ought to be getting hold of the under tens by taking them pond-dipping in the close season. That is the time to get them, to begin their instruction. I reckon it would start them out in exactly the right direction. I can imagine too that parents and schools would welcome the involvement of angling clubs in this way. It would not be too long before those youngsters graduated to angling, either by asking the club officials or by doing it themselves, with their friends. But however they begin they will already have a good grounding.

Of course, there's no good reason why the clubs shouldn't charge the parents for such guidance of their offspring. If your child is into karate you have to spend several hundred pounds per annum for their weekly fees, clothes examinations etc. Note I said several hundred pounds, not 2.00 for a licence or ticket.

Today's karate kids will have a knowledge of and respect for the rest of their lives, even if they choose to do something else eventually. It would be nice if the sport of angling was underpinned in the same way. But it isn't. We put in minimal effort on behalf of our youngsters. Unlike other sports the youthful angler does need a lot of time to himself, fishing, but we as adults in clubs could do a great deal more to help both the children and the future of the sport.

And so the young Rickards stumbled along by himself, eventually landing a small perch, deep hooked. But that didn't matter because it was taken home and fried. He never forgot that first occasion when the float was no more. When the line went taut from rod tip to the pond weed-bed, and how the bristling perch was pulled out, trailing a length of weed stem. It wasn't a perch of Venablesian proportions, but it looked good on the kitchen table - and in the pan. And it ate well, as perch do.

The next thing he discovered was spinning. A peer was into spinning, and the young Rickards bumped into him one day. That too was never forgotten. And, looking back, it was a great pity that he didn't take up spinning at once. For starters it is a very active part of the sport: no chance of an impatient youth becoming bored. Not only that, but all the casting means that spinning soon makes you a proficient caster, especially when different sizes and types of lure are used. And the fish, though less frequent than small rudd, weigh a pound or two at least. A lot of water is covered, new vistas unfolding by the minute - and always the chance of a real whopper. Taken all in all I reckon that spinning is a method that youngsters ought to be taught fairly quickly. An afternoon is enough to get them fairly competent: contrast that with the time needed with light float work or fly-fishing.

We do not know what makes a youngster stick with angling. We know why many teenagers do a bit of angling. It's the same hunting urge that took many of them pond-dipping on their own, without help or guidance. But a very successful young fisherman is just as likely to give it up as a poor angler. Indeed, it often seems to me that the most unlikely pupils are the ones who persist. So it has to be the atmosphere, the ethos of angling, not the catching of fish. And we can help prepare anglers to enjoy that atmosphere if we do not take too seriously the need to catch fish. For myself I know it all started in physical terms. But, emotionally, I had already been "done" as it were, because I had excellent tutoring in pond-dipping, and a deep interest in natural history that has never waned. After pond-dipping I was largely self taught - except for Venables, and Walker and . . . for, by then, I could read as well as fish. The influence of the writers and the fishing magazines had a greater effect on me than personal instruction. Most adults then, as now, had little interest in helping a youngster. And of the writers you soon learned who were the angler-writers and who were the armchair anglers. There is something almost indefinable about the written word of a real fisher as opposed to one who doesn't fish. And there is something indefinable about the atmosphere of a day by the water, when an old and experienced hand is allowing the young man to learn: by gently guiding; by not pushing; by allowing the youth to succeed - or not - by his own efforts.

The Shark

By Sarah Bruty

Sharks are very horrible things,
How I wonder if they play on swings.
Are they fond of fish and chips?
Really, how I wonder.

Pond Dipping

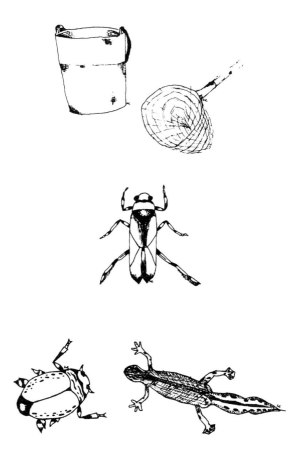

By Jodi Bestwick

We were walking round the wood and went to the pond. We got out the nets and a bucket and put water in it. As we put the nets into the water I could see a beetle swimming along. I caught it and put it in the bucket and it swam about like a bird flying in the sky. It looked as though it was trying to jump out.

I left it and went back to the pond to see what else was there. I fished out a ball of grass which looked like a football and had been kicked into the pond. I saw a tadpole, caught it and put it in the bucket to swim about. I could see the two little legs kicking. There were some more things in the bucket such as something like a fish with no tail and four legs.

It was time to go home so I put everything back.

A Love Affair

By Charles Jardine

I can't quite recall whether it was the impetus of a strike or my precarious position on a decidedly rickety seat that sent me into an inelegant parabola backwards into stagnant, decaying mud. However, I emerged struggling, little hands still clutching the rod with the tenacity of a lion cub, looking for all the world like Winnie the Pooh masquerading, mud covered, as a small dark cloud.

I knew my prize was not attached where the books - pored over in murky light - suggested it would be.

That was one of my earliest recollections of tench fishing failure. My apprenticeship - as with so many others - was spent in pursuit of toothsome torpedoes lurking amid ochre clad reeds; winter was the time of pike. Those striped cavaliers, full of gusto and dash, the perch, were our mainstay throughout the year. The delicate pearly roach was autumn's harvest, for we eager floatfishers the Kentish Stour seemed to come alive in October and November with these elegant fish.

Yet summer, and all the idylls of school holidays belonged to the tench - there were always rudd, but tench held the mind - they always seemed an unobtainable dream. The fish that everyone else caught - not me.

I tried for years. Even when, two years earlier, at the age of six, I landed my first trout, the tench clouded summer horizons like a threatening storm cloud. Mr Crabtree, Fred J. Taylor, Dick Walker all told me "how"; what they omitted was "when".

A big problem to a small mind grows "like Topsy", soon failure permeates the very pores. In piscatorial company, a small head drops on dropped shoulders. The flaw in your fishing dogs your piscatorial steps especially when in the company of fishing friends - a pariah amidst your peers. Even the greedily digested, then embryonic Angling Times, Creel, Angling magazines - sage words spilling from every page - further emphasised the failure; everyone else caught tench and I didn't.

The trouble when one is small (7,8 or 9 years) is that ones whole vista becomes clouded - a case of not seeing "the wood for the trees". Of course, what I should have been doing (so easy with 30 odd years' hindsight), was seeking out such waters where tench lived, not just the odd tench, but so many they would look like a multi-storey car park full of the darned things.

In my innocence, I felt every water to be a tench water and that churlishly they were located everywhere that I wasn't. Simple.

The "tide turned" one evening at a private lake just outside Ashford. My late father was known to be able to bribe anyone where fishing was concerned; and so it was, on that lake - the talk of legendary carp may have had something to do with it.

My preparation was fastidious - lines, float, shot, hooks - everything checked, arranged and re-arranged with the type of fervour and angst that only a small angler knows. I got bait - and what bait it was! Lobworms, the size of small snakes; Brandlings out of a heady encounter with the compost heap; paste that had driven mother potty in the kitchen; maggots, whose bid for escape had only been halted by the fridge door.

Mother deposited us by the ruined chapel, father and I picked our way through the knotted darkening foliage to a small peninsular, jutting rather like a hammer head into the main bowl of the lake. Father picked a reed strewn swim at the far end and encamped me in a mid-section, a gap flanked by satanic cedar trees - dark and intimidating. Yet, ahead lay a crystal avenue of uninterrupted water, similarly flanked, but by welcoming lily pads, great joyful rafts of them. This was good - I had read that tench love lily pads. This was my Nirvana.

My reel was a well run-in Starback type. The rod, an Appollo tubular steel Taperflash - outmoded, but serviceable. Not perhaps the height of sophistication, but in those days a passable stab at "street cred" for a youngster. The float was wonderful, gently curved swan quill, crafted by an angling friend, who knew nothing of thrift and had painstakingly put whipping thread along its length. It really was a work of art. I still have it and covet it.

Trembling fingers sped the impaled worm into the channel. Having done my stuff, checked depth and adjusted my float tackle - the worm now seductively lurking at the bottom - thrown out a few chopped worms (I was never squeamish, thank heaven), and generally appraised and "cased the joint", I nestled back into my little fold-away wooden seat and waited. I waited until I could not wait any longer. And, let's face it, even an ardent angler gets bored.

I resisted. Periodically my hand would dart towards the rod rest, some inner voice dragging it back, I must have waited a full quarter of an hour before I re-cast. This time a fraction closer to the lilies than intended.

The night sky was now in the ascendant and clambering all over the pure blues of early evening with dark fading to peach and pearl. The water darkened too.

My attention was dragged from the now crescendo of silence about me, to a chain of incandescent bubbles the size of match heads coursing along the channel. Chain links of them, hither and thither like serpentine coils.

The gathering silence of night was now screaming. A bird or animal rustled nearby. I shot out of my skin. Yet settled quickly back in my sepulchral igloo.

The bubbles were a steady profusion. That meant something. I knew that, but what? Sure, I had read that tench "bubbled", but somehow that notion seemed a vague, forlorn hope which I didn't dare think about.

Night was gathering its momentum into inky oblivion. The water reflected the silvery overhead threads, alternating crimson and purple. The float a dark motionless shape. Did it move? Transfixed; the point of my fixation, the float glided into the left-hand side lilies, wobbled, dipped and vanished. I knew something had got that worm.

Almost detached from the whole thing, I struck. I struck as though my life depended on that one act. A solid thing tugged back.

I was not going to lose that fish, that I decided. Mr Crabtree told Peter "sidestrain" - I did as the strip cartoon suggested. Mr Venables' further bidding had taught the importance of constant pressure - the line hummed like a finely tuned instrument. Grudgingly the immovable moved.

It was then that I experienced for the first time the adrenalin rush that is the quintessence of the sport. It made the senses soar then and has continued to do so. The headlong run of a fish - its first unstoppable run is the very essence of our sport.

I was in awe. Both of us unbowed, see-sawed in "give and take". I knew I would win. I had to, young pride would not tolerate failure.

There is that time in a fight when some primeval sense tells you that you are the victor, capitulation of your quarry is near. And so it was.

My net lay waiting like a meshed cavern. The dark shape sank in to it.

I called for father.

In the light of the torch, the ruby eye solemnly held mine as mesmerised as any cobra. The olive tiny scaled bulk and fleshy paddle-like fins, filled my senses. The "grail" had been found.

My first tench, caressed in my tiny hands, slipped noiselessly back into the indigo water. I had "come of age" as a fisher.

Many years have passed; my long standing love affair with game fish remains undiminished. Yet each summer my thoughts are with tench. When I don't answer the childhood call, my fishing will then be over.

I Can Still See Every Spot On It

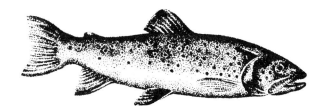

By Steve Parton

Technically, I've lived on borrowed time for the past thirty years. When I was seven a slight ache turned into appendicitis, my dad rushed me to The Children's Hospital and I got lucky. I was trouble and the doctors discharged me as early as they could. Suddenly I got six weeks off school and only one restriction,

"Don't swing on trees."

It was late summer with autumn coming fast and I spent the first weeks curled up in a corner by the fire reading and reading. Reading all sorts of books, grown up books I had to re-read many times over the coming years. Books that changed meaning as I grew up and found out about the other things in life like faithlessness, villainy, sex and death. Foremost amongst the books was a late 1880's copy of The Compleat Angler.

It was heavily annotated. In fact the notes were far more interesting than the text, which left me convinced that old man Walton knew less than I did about fishing, and that was even before I was a fisherman. And still I think I knew more about fishing as a child than ever he did as a grown man, even now so much later, and still I love what he wrote. A cousin borrowed that book years after and it never came back and I wish I could lay my hands on the original and re-read it just one more time.

The book started me. Before I went back to school, thinner and taller after the convalescence, I'd managed to dig worms, buy two hooks, borrow the rod and line that used to go with one of those light plastic aeroplanes which had revolving wings (it was maybe a foot long overall) and I went fishing. I went to the local canal and sneaked up to the edge and lowered my baited hook down and the magic started. It was a warm grey drizzly afternoon and I had 22 bites all from perch, I could see them too, and I never hooked one but they hooked me.

My dad never did encourage me or my sister in sports. His father never encouraged him and I don't encourage my children. It is the best way, start yourself and never let go. And don't lose the proportion or wonder of fishing and it won't overtake your life the way tennis and gymnastic kids get lost and twisted out of childhoods.

Dad was the key to fly-fishing though, even though he never fished himself or ever wanted to. A couple of years after I started at the canal and before I'd caught anything he went to some dinner and sat next to a proper fisherman. And the following Christmas I got an old Allcock's Silver Two split-cane rod, reel, a silk line and Wiggin's "Teach Yourself Fly Fishing" and Wilcock's "Come Fly Fishing With Me". And an invitation to go to D & P Batteries water at Bakewell on Easter Monday following to fish for trout with Invictas.

When I got there four months later I was keyed up. The books were thumbed and grubby, I still couldn't really cast but I could tie knots. I had six Invictas and three Ginger Quill nymphs, I had Mucilin and Luron Two nylon line. The water we fished was like a little canal. Slightly up the hill from the main Wye, no doubt built with its little accompanying lake to drive some waterwheel in the Industrial Revolution. It is still there but I have never been back, I think maybe I never should. It will have shrunk away to something small and insignificant where once it was a giant stage.

I remember catching up a lot in rhubarb like weeds on the back cast and after that I remember seeing the first trout. It was working steadily along the weed-beds. I watched it patrol up and down and it seemed so obvious to sneak up to the top of the beat and cast out ready for it. As it passed me heading up towards my nymph I lost sight of it in the surface glare but I pulled the fly towards where I thought it was and it took me hard. The reel screeched twice and the hook came away, I sat down and cried.

Since then I have lost many more things that meant much less than that fish. Factories closed, girls lost interest, jobs went, friends vanished after school and university, the odd business disappeared, they filled in my canal, good companions died and hard times came, went and came again. My dad is old now and I am no longer young.

Mum always wanted me to have a safe job in government with a pension and security. Dad worried about his future and he was a professor. Then the bike works fell in onto itself and I escaped and now have a fishing tackle shop; I am not wealthy but damn, it is fun. There is almost nothing connected with fly-fishing that either I can't do or have no working knowledge of. I learned to make rods, reels, lines, flies and many accessories; I write a little and I design and specify fishing tackle for a major company. I've got a lovely wife and three kids and even a grandson. Maybe I've ruined my life, it certainly doesn't feel like it.

The fishing has always been there with me right from the small boy weeping on the bank. It always was my private world, the place I worked to be at, what I lived to do. When I fish everything else fades. I can't do it more than twice a week, I have to rest between the intense little episodes. It has taken me to odd places I would never otherwise have got to. Alaska, Colorado, Florida, Shakhalin at the end of the Communist Empire and most of Europe. You wouldn't believe some of the tons of fish I've caught over the last thirty five years. You wouldn't believe most of the friends I've caught them with, either. All my friends are fishermen, all the close ones that is. Maybe I don't know real people anymore or maybe I don't know the real ones. I suspect that if you don't fish then you are not yourself real in any meaningful way. Most of the Nazarene's pals were fishermen and can you fault them for that? I can't. He might fault me for my politics though; the way I see it is, if the trout are lost you smash the state. All I want is money to support my family and time enough to fish. Otherwise the authorities have a major problem.

If I close my eyes and think back I can still see every spot on that trout. Why should that be? What would have happened if I'd actually landed it? Maybe I'd would have gone looking for other worlds to conquer, I don't know.

Perhaps it is best to lose the first real fish, perhaps it is better not to be a fisherman at all. I wouldn't really change anything in my life, even a little thing like a trout that threw a hook. My life maybe hinges around the small boy who lost that trout; I think I'm still trying my damndest to catch it though it's long gone this thirty five years.

The Little Boy With Fishes

By Moc Morgan

It was the morning of the annual carnival and the whole village was buzzing. I was busy decorating a huge lorry that was to carry our tableau depicting the necessity of protecting the environment. We considered it to be an ideal tableau as a certain section of the land near the village had been designated a nature reserve. I was to dress up as the local squire with a gundog and gun. Most of my mates from the second year group in secondary school were also in the scene.

We were looking forward to an enjoyable afternoon riding around the village on the back of the lorry. Then it happened. The lady who had the task of co-ordinating the carnival efforts of our street, called on my mother. The affair was organised as an inter-street competition. I heard her ask my mother if I could help by getting a brace of trout as one little boy was to dress as a disciple with five loaves and two fishes for the feeding of the multitude.

Mam, bless her, said that I would. I received my orders to go and catch a brace of trout; I needed no second bidding.

Off I went, confident that it would take me but a few minutes. I went to the Brenig, a tributary of the Teifi, only some fifty yards from our house. I started to fish with the dry fly. Although only thirteen, I had been fishing for four years and was pretty good with the dry. In the first pool, which we kids used for swimming, I cast the fly into the neck and watched it float down with the current. As the fly came round the bend I saw it disappear and tightened the line. The fish was on and very quickly I brought it to the bank: a nice brown of about one pound. A good start I thought, confident that soon I would be back to help decorate the lorry. I was disappointed that the Concrete Pool, as it was called, did not produce another fish.

On I went to the next pool, known as John's Pool; much to my surprise, I failed to rise one fish. I could hardly believe that I had failed to take a trout from the best pool on the river. On to the next pool with a small weir at its neck where I cast my fly quite accurately behind a large stone below the fall. Not a single fish showed any interest in my offering.

Doubts began to enter my mind. I had been so confident that I would have my brace by now. So on I went to the next pool which held big trout in the riffle at its narrow section. I cast over every inch of that stretch and got no response whatsoever.

Now I began to fear that I would not get the fish after all. The next pool was under the small bridge that spanned the river in the middle of the village. A few people leaned over and shouted their greetings; I had no time for them. In a deep run under the far bank I watched the fly come floating down and to my delight I saw a fish take it. I tightened, hooked the fish and reeled in. Disappointment followed when I saw that it was far too small, about seven inches. I was about to put it back when something stopped me; I decided to keep it - just in case.

I fished for the next hour up along the river but failed to get anything to show interest in my fly. I now realised that I would require some sort of miracle to enable me to catch a decent sized trout.

Unfortunately after two hours of hard fishing I still had not got the brace I needed and time was running short. I still had to go and get myself ready for the carnival.

I worked my way back to where I had started and once again tried the Concrete Pool, right in the spot where I had met with success. A big fish came up and took the fly. Much to my frustration the damn thing threw the hook as I was reeling in. There was nothing for it but to go back with two very badly matched trout; I thought that the miracle would look even more impressive with one of the fish being so very small.

Mother dismissed my effort with a query as to why it had taken me so long!

The little boy dressed in his biblical guise and cradling five loaves and a brace of ill-matched fish in his arms did not win a prize in the carnival that afternoon. A disappointment not only to him but also his mother and to me. The judge obviously had no idea of the effort involved in the preparation of that disciple.

The carnival judge did not receive the brace of fish for his supper as promised.

After all, you cannot reward inefficiency - even in a judge!

A Lesson For All Of Us

By Bernard Aldrich

The Broadlands Estate has always had a policy of co-operating with local schools in educating young people to be aware of the countryside environment and the animal and fish life that inhabit it. As Fisheries Manager of the estate I have been involved with the schools project mainly with children in the 5-11 age group.

The parties of children arrive at my fishing hut where I give a short talk describing the river, lakes, management, stocking policies and maintenance. Then we pile the kids into a tractor and trailer and give them a bumpy ride upstream, stopping now and then to point out items of interest. The journey stops at our fish farm where the children feed the fish and ask any questions they may have. I sometimes get to see written projects produced as a result of the visit; often, the most memorable part of the trip seems to be the tractor ride!

The Cedar School visit holds special memories for me. I first visited the school to talk to the pupils in preparation for their project "The River Test". Having discovered that it was a special school for the disabled and handicapped children I felt a little nervous about addressing such a group: I need not have worried. They were super kids, very interested in all I had to say and specially keen to examine the rods, reels and flies that I had taken to demonstrate fishing techniques.

The question and answer session went on for so long that my talk over-ran the allotted time. When they finally let me go I had tea with the head teacher and I asked if it would be possible to transport small groups of children to the river so that they could see for themselves what went on. The school owns a mini-bus adapted for carrying wheelchairs, so it was just a question of whether the vehicle could negotiate our riverside tracks. I took the driver to the river and showed him the proposed route. He was a lovely man and saw no problems with this.

We had decided to arrange the outing in two groups on separate days. I later learned from a teacher that there had been much vying for position from the youngsters claiming various forms of priority. Age and severity of disability were taken into consideration as they argued about who should go on the first trip.

My staff and I completed as much preparation as possible for the visit, mowing grass and filling potholes around the fish farm to ease the progress of wheelchairs. We had also made up many plastic bags of trout food for the children to feed the fish.

Came the great day! There was much excitement as the children were loaded aboard the bus. Some were wheelchair bound, some on crutches or with walking sticks, but all enthusiastic about the journey and very happy.

It took us nearly half-an-hour to disembark and distribute them along the fence surrounding the fish-rearing ponds. I think that they were a little disappointed at first as there were no signs of fish life or activity in the water. The fish of course were lying doggo, upset by all the disturbance that can only be created by a group of noisy children. Each pupil was given their bag of trout food and told to wait for the word "go" before throwing handfuls of pellets into the pond.

On the word of command they threw their first salvo and the pond erupted as four thousand large trout overcame their nervousness and began to feed, leaping and splashing and soaking many of the excited children in the process. They enjoyed it immensely and once more the time schedule went by the board as we doled out further supplies of food. Eventually, we tore the boys and girls away; tired and weary they returned to the school.

The second trip, in the same format as the first, was also enjoyed by all. At the last moment two children in wheelchairs came forward. There was a pretty little blond girl and an angelic looking boy, both about ten years of age with badly disabled hands and arms. They asked me,

"What is your favourite food?"

I had been warned by a teacher that this question would be asked: I had my reply ready.

"Trout, I loved stuffed trout."

Their little faces lit up as they produced two carrier bags which they presented to me. In the first bag there was a beautifully made cardboard trout, correct in all detail and painted in bright colours. The other bag contained a long piece of string with fronds of brown and green crepe paper hanging from it, this was to represent the weeds growing in the river.

With great ceremony the weed was duly hung across my fishing hut with the trout "swimming" in the middle. Later, I was told that it had taken the youngsters over six hours to make and paint that trout. I was deeply moved. That trout is one of my most treasured possessions taking pride of place in my fishing hut. Working with these wonderful children and their devoted staff was one of the most rewarding experiences of my life.

We now have an annual fishing event for handicapped children on our lakes. Local fishing clubs send their members along. Each brings his own tackle and bait and is partnered with a child for the day to show them how to fish. We usually stock the lake with trout before the visit to ensure that the children catch plenty of fish. The day ends with a barbecue before a lot of very sleepy youngsters are taken home.

These are happy days, looked forward to and enjoyed by all who take part. Long may they continue.

Hooked

By Chris Ogborne

Everyone seems to remember their first fish very clearly, but fly-fishing has been part of my life for so long that I'm ashamed to say that all those early fish tend to blur into one lovely, long, lingering memory of youth. Looking back is invariably a case of rose-tinted specs, but even with that amount of licence I know with great certainty that my childhood was both coloured and enriched by fishing.

Indeed, fly-fishing has shaped much of my adult life as well as those early days. With fishing came a love of the countryside, an affinity with the nature and wildlife of the Mendip Hills, and a deep fascination with bird watching. No man can call himself an angler without at least some degree of appreciation of his surroundings: if bird and animal life are little more than background then he is no true fisher.

I am especially lucky in that my father is also a lifelong fisherman, and in many ways it was inevitable that he should pass his feeling for the countryside to me. Childhood was spent in and around those Mendip Hills - our family could never have survived in town - and Chew Valley Lake was then, as it is now, my playground. It was directly because of Chew that I changed from being a mere angler, and turned to the most fascinating and rewarding of all the branches of this great sport: fly-fishing.

An uncle in Sweden used to make an annual pilgrimage to England, ostensibly to visit the family.

Dad and I knew the real reason: yes, he spent the odd hour doing the duty calls to relatives, but what he really came for was the fishing. In those days before the stillwater boom of the '60s, Chew was very much under-fished and it was a veritable paradise. My uncle was able to practice his favourite dry fly tactics undisturbed.

I had been using worm and float for my trout up until then, but when after much pestering and cajoling I was allowed to accompany them on one of their trips, the foundations were well and truly laid. I was fascinated and a little in awe of this wonderfully fluid casting action: the gentle unfurling line, and the supreme delicacy of the flies themselves would have been enough. But to see the point of contact, to witness the moment when the tiny fly was engulfed by a confident head-and-tail only to be followed by galvanitic action and an explosion of spray - yes, I was well and truly hooked!

The learning curve that followed was dramatic. My uncle lent me an old rod to practice with, and returned to Sweden with a promise that if I could cast a fly to his satisfaction by the time he returned the following year then he would kit me out more thoroughly. Had I been at the airport when he landed I would probably have dragged him to the nearest strip of grass, but in the event I had to wait at least three days whilst he "did the rounds" of the family. Only then was I able to demonstrate how I could hit the handkerchief with the fly about six times out of ten at ten metres range.

True to his word he took me straight to the shops, and only then did the real lessons start. As so many people know, casting is one thing but fishing is very much another. His patience, and that of my father gradually put the meat on the bones of raw casting. At school we were lucky enough to have the Midford Brook running through the grounds. The wild browns were a real test, and by the time I left school and became a management trainee (a desirable title in those days!), I was more than ready for Chew.

Oh the glories of living at home as a trainee! Home every evening at six, wait for half-an-hour till dad got in, and then drag him off to Chew before mum could even think about offering us dinner. Long velvet summer evenings were rounded off by a pint or two on the way home. Most times we stayed until dark, or at least until the rise had died away. It was now 1967, my first season ticket on the Bristol waters (paid for by dad, with my everlasting gratitude) and it was the purest magic.

In days of early youth it seems that parents are seldom appreciated. But with the beginnings of commercial awareness, and the hard lesson that each pound spent needs first to be earned, the help with that season ticket meant so much. Dad and I became closer, far more so than could be the case with a non-fishing father and son; we established a genuine friendship that has never since been bettered.

Since those days we have reinforced the friendship a thousand times, with days on bank and boat, river and lake, and in fair weather or foul. We have tied flies side by side - I even sold them in the winter to pay for the next year's season ticket - and we have made a video together. We have shared many fish together, and probably many bottles of wine at lunchtime to the detriment of afternoon casting, but it is all part of the rich tapestry that has been in the weaving for thirty years.

Dad has retired now, and I enjoy the ultimate pleasure of returning the compliment and paying for his fishing. This wonderful sport has been kind to me, and I am now able to take dad on days that would have been little more than pipe dreams to us in those early days. We have been to the mighty River Test together, fished boats on exclusive private waters, and more recently we have previewed Roadford Lake - a pilgrimage that may never be repeated.

But beyond those famous named waters, with all their great pedigree, I suspect that for dad it would still be the memories of those halcyon days at Chew and Blagdon that hold a special slot in the memory. The evenings went on for ever, with burgundy sunsets over Blagdon's dam or the lovely Chew Valley fading into a soft mist at dusk. There were evenings then when we never bothered to fish: we just watched the swifts wheel into the fading light, until their screaming song was drowned by the altitude and the owls in the distance said that it was time for home. Even in his 70s dad is still a young man, and in those days of my late teens he was frequently referred to as "your friend" or "your mate down the bank" much to his amusement and, I suspect, to his secret pleasure.

A pleasure shared is automatically a pleasure that grows in strength, and because of my dad my fishing has always had that extra edge. I re-live competition days with him, and share memories of trips abroad to fabled waters. Only a fisherman can understand the joys of another fisherman, but when you share an empathy for the countryside as well as a bloodline then that sharing is so much more special, more intense.

Age is little more than a state of mind, and dad is in no way "old". As I approach my own middle age I suppose I should be slowing down a little but, apart from the extra inches at the waistline, there are only a few signs of the years. Dad and I still get the buzz when Opening Day comes around in April, and each of us thrills to the first fish of the day, no matter which one of us catches it. If, as the saying goes, days spent fishing are not subtracted from ones allotted span, then we both have many, many more years ahead of us. Together. Fishing.

Jaws 5½
Florida To Alaska

By Matthew Smith

One day Jeremy Beadle went on a fishing holiday in Florida. As he was walking down the street everybody was screaming,

"AAAAAAHHHHHH! it's Beadle. Hide. Watch out. Beadle's about."

So he hired a boat and sped out to sea and cast out his tackle. TWANG - went the line. SSSSSSCCCCCCRRRRRR went the reel as he pulled up a three foot skate. The skate said,

"AAAAAAHHHHHH Beadle's about."

He unhooked himself and dived back in.

CRRRRRUUNNNCH went the front half of the boat. Then his line went straight.

"AAAAAAHHHHHH!" he shouted as he went flying through the air. Then he was in the water. He was going so fast that he was water skiing in trainers.

"Slow down!"

He travelled for two whole days until he reached Alaska where officials rescued him.

The Colonel

(A true story)

By John Hatherell

The drone of a single enemy aircraft interrupted the tenor of a hot summer's day. A lone boy was attaching boiled hempseed to a small hook by the side of the Kennet overlooking the quiet village of Thatcham in Berkshire. Work on the new Ordnance Depot nearby was interrupted by the sound of the air raid sirens and the workers moved into the shelters. The boy watched the scene with dispassionate interest; up on the canal it was unlikely that there would be any danger.

The Dornier aeroplane was so low that the pilots were quite visible in the cockpit. Strange, thought the boy, that the anti-aircraft guns were silent; he was not to know that because of the close proximity of friendly aircraft to the depot no orders could be given for the guns to open fire.

At the canal side of the depot two army bungalows were being constructed. One was already occupied by the depot's temporary commanding officer. The Colonel was a very keen fisherman and only the previous evening he and the boy were talking together

about the large chub the boy had just returned to the
water. On a number of occasions the Colonel had
shown the boy his fly box filled with drab coloured
small flies tied onto very small hooks. Each fly had
been lovingly made by the Colonel from various
feathers and wool. Perhaps one day I shall try and catch
fish with an artificial fly, thought the boy.

His attention was returned sharply to the German
aircraft; a machine gun was making little puffs of white
smoke on the asbestos roof of the depot: still no one
returned fire. Then from the bungalow out rushed the
Colonel. With pistol he fired at the enemy aeroplane.
It was like aiming dried peas from a peashooter at a
charging elephant. The aircraft turned again but this
time its guns were silent. A large dark bomb dropped
from the floor of the aircraft and began its slow descent
towards the depot - towards the spot where the Colonel
was standing. The boy crouched riveted to the ditch
that he had moved to when the shooting began. It was
like watching a film at the local cinema, the whole scene
seemed unreal. The bomb hit a huge pile of sand and
gravel next to the nearly finished bungalow and just
where the Colonel was standing. There was a great
orange flash and a big plume of brown debris. His friend
could never have known what had happened. One
bungalow was flattened completely and the other had
no roof. A tear fell from the cheek of the boy, his own
big brother had been killed leaving the French port of

Dunkerque only a few months ago, and he felt very alone all of a sudden.

Mr Varley, the Station Master was hurrying towards him,

"Come along John, your mum is worried about you and it's time for tea."

The boy never knew the name of his friend who had been so kind and generous but he would always remember him as "The Colonel".

I Remember

"try that," said the boy

By J.H.A.S. Bean

"Blast it!" said the fisherman, as he gazed mournfully at his slack line and the hole in the water where his specimen trout head been. Pulling in his line, he saw the curly pig-tail of nylon which proved a poor tying of the knot. The evening shadows had lengthened, and there was a distinct chill in the air. A little shudder went through him.

"I shall not set up again," he thought. "Another half hour and I shan't be able to see to tie the fly. Might as well have a leisurely stroll back along the river bank to the pub."

Trout were beginning to rise all over the stretch of river, sipping in sedges as a never-ending carpet of them moved towards the rising fish.

The fisherman became aware that he was under scrutiny. Quickly turning, he saw a young boy gazing steadily at him.

"Now's the time, sir, now's the time to catch your fish."

A wave of irritation went through the angler.

"Yes I know," he said evenly, trying not to show his feeling. "I have just lost a good trout, and decided to give 'em best for tonight."

"I know ," said the boy. "I saw you lose him."

The fisherman's eyes hardened for an instant; the boy shuffled a step closer.

"There's a better fish than the one you lost under the old willow, in that pool a few yards further up."

The man looked keenly at the boy. Was there something vaguely familiar about him? He judged that he was telling the truth.

"O.K.," he said, "show me."

The boy led the way along the tow-path for a short distance, and then stopped.

"There he is," he said, pointing to a long dark shape in the water.

"A huge fish," thought the fisherman. "Perhaps as much as five pounds." The hunter's instinct welled up inside him and he quickly tied on another dark sedge pattern. The fish was feeding steadily, but totally ignored the fisherman's offering. The boy gazed on.

"You don't seem to have the right fly," he said. "I could let you have one."

"I'm sure there is no need to use your flies," said the fisherman petulantly. "I have plenty that I haven't tried yet."

"Be dark soon," observed the boy.

Taking a hook from his pocket and a thread from his jersey he carefully wound the thread on to the hook. Searching around, he found a mallard breast-feather lying in a tuft of grass. With deft fingers he tore a few fibres from the feather and tied them along the hook shank. From this ragged dark green trousers another thread was torn and wound on to form a thorax. The fisherman looked on with interest and a faint stirring of uneasy memory.

"Who taught you to dress flies like that?" he asked.

"A friend," said the boy uncommunicatively.

At last the fly was finished.

"Try that," said the boy.

The fisherman gazed at the offering critically.

"It looks a bit big," he said at last.

"No," said the boy, "he'll take that all right."

"You try it then," said the fisherman.

"O.K." said the boy, and, taking the rod, quickly tied on his fly. With a well judged cast he landed the fly three feet above the feeding fish. There was a swirl, and the fly disappeared.

"God bless us all," the boy muttered, and tightened on to the fish.

"You've got him! Well done!" cried the man in wonder; and then rather enviously added, "I bet he goes five pounds at least."

"Four pounds ten ounces," grunted the boy, as he battled with the giant fish.

By now darkness had fallen, and the fish could only just be seen as it moved up and down the pool.

"He must tire soon," said the fisherman.

"Yes, you'd think so," said the boy.

A thought struck the angler.

"How do you know the weight of this fish," he asked, with growing unease.

"Oh, we're old friends," said the lad, with an odd smile, and again turned the fish's head away from the weed-bed.

"What's your name?" asked the fisherman urgently.

"Joe Bland," replied the boy.

"But that's my name," said the fisherman. "I don't understand. . . ."

"Mr Bland! Mr Bland!"

A voice came through the darkness.

"Mr Bland! Are you there? Are you all right?"

"Over here," said the fisherman. "I'm over here."

"We were getting quite worried about you, out so late in the dark." It was the landlord from the pub.

"Oh I'm all right, we were just landing a big fish, any minute now!" He turned to see how his young friend was doing.

The pool was empty, except for a large and beautiful fish feeding steadily under the old willow.

"Let's go back to the pub, this part of the river always give me the creeps," said the landlord.

"Yes," said the fisherman, "it always did, ever since I was a lad and used to fish here on my holidays. I remember now. . . ."

Magical Days

A conversation with
Brian Leadbetter

Bill Hood, better known to his friends as Methusala to those amongst us who had come under his spell, was one of the real old school of fishermen. He was always smartly turned out for his fishing trips. Resplendent in his dark grey suit , three piece of course, and with watch and chain across his middle, he would wander down to the river nearly every day.

I came into the world in a house a short distance from the centre of the town of Bedford. We lived just two hundred yards from the River Ouse and two doors up from Bill. With master, student and classroom all in such close proximity, my destiny was assured. From an early age I was taking full advantage of the free fishing so close at hand. The clear, slow moving river with its deep and inviting weirpools was really full of fish at that time. Quality roach, bream and chub shoaled densely in this beautiful stretch of water.

My father wasn't interested in river fishing. He preferred the call of the sea. He insisted that until I had my swimming certificate, solo trips were out of the question. So I had to seek the company of lads from my street and go down to the river with them. We youngsters had our uses. During the pike season we were fully occupied catching livebait for the older boys.

So it was that under Bill's watchful eye that I discovered how to use my eleven foot rod of Spanish reed to catch those Ouse fish. That rod was built by him to very high standards. It lasted well and I have it to this day. The rest of my tackle was purchased at Dixon Brothers' shop in Bedford. That piece of angling history has also survived. Old Bill would never use worms or maggots. He preferred bread, cheese or wheat for bait. He would often take some of his catch home, not for some fat cat: to cook for his own dinner.

Of course with boys being boys, us lads eventually began to roam further afield. We were lured downstream by some fantastic chub. Perhaps we got an extra thrill from the fact they were often to be found holed up in private waters. Not that we were put off by such minor hazards as signs that declared: "FISHING FORBIDDEN" and "TRESPASSERS WILL BE PROSECUTED". Once captured by the owner, it was a resounding smack round the ear and a menacing, "And don't come back again!" that sent us on our way.

It is sad but true that at that time we just did not realise what heaven we had in that stretch of water. It is still free fishing but that is about all that remains the same. The river has been dredged and become more like a canal. That, of course, is to provide free passage for the many cabin cruisers. This process has destroyed most of the spawning beds and the stocks have been drastically reduced.

What would Methusala make of it all? I hope that he would be able to work some magic to restore this stretch of the Ouse to its former glory. Perhaps restore it to those times when we really could sit and pull out fish all day long.

Fisher Among Men

By Nick Fisher

There's not much I remember about being five. I remember I broke my foot by dropping a paving stone on it in my dad's garage. I remember my big sister making me eat mud. And I remember my first fish.

It was all mine. No adult intervention. No grown up holding up the rod, hooking a fish then passing it to me. This was MY fish. Fought and caught, fair and square.

It was a family holiday in Scotland. My dad had the fishing gear with him and had firm intentions of wetting his tackle. I nagged him to get a rod. In the end, I got one, from somewhere deeply naff like Woolworths.

It was a kiddy fishing kit. I knew it wasn't real. Although the bright red plasticky bits looked nice, I knew, even at that age, there was some con going on. This wasn't kosher like my dad had. This was some playful imitation. But hey, it was a fishing rod.

So, next thing I knew we were on a rocky pier in Millport and my dad and a few other blokes were casting their real rods, sending complicated terminal tackle miles out on the horizon. Meanwhile, my comedy kid's joke rod had no casting function whatsoever. It was simply plonk it straight down - or don't. That was the choice.

So with the sickest looking lugworm out of the paper wrapping, because my dad didn't want to waste any good bait, and a hook which came free with the rod and was way to big, I plonked.

I was happy to be fishing, but I knew then I was not playing on the same pitch as the menfolk. They had great gear. Stuff like waders, big penknives, filleting knives, Tilley lamps, metal buckets and rod stands. I had a plastic rod.

I was fishing, but I knew I was being had. It didn't help when some patronising git who thought he had a way with kids came and fibbed me how I'd do much better close in than way out like the others.

This is a bit like nailing Andre Agassi's feet to the floor then telling him what a great game table tennis is.

After a long while, nothing happened. Nothing happened for me, but more to the point, nothing happened for the menfolk. Zilch. Nada. Nothing.

So of course they started to moan. They all leaned over the rail together, my dad included, and shared their considered and nonsensical notions as to why the fishing was crap.

Then someone got a bite. A vibrating, nibblesome knock at the end of one of their rods. And it was as though Lulu had just suddenly appeared naked before them. They all stood round, open-mouthed watching this one rod tip, immersed in anticipation.

Just then, the joke rod in my hands bent like a half a hoola hoop. Then the hi-kitsch 60's Winfield plastic reel made a horrible noise it was never meant to make. Like a fast revving Flymo hitting a sack of gravel.

I squeaked and yelped. Nobody paid any attention. My dad told me to shush. And they stared at the Lulu-esque rod tip.

I tried to wind and make some line. I managed a bit. Both reel and me then competed to see who could make the highest pitch squeal. As bits of plastic collapsed between my fingers and line went back and forth like a yo-yo trick, one of the menfolk took his eyes off Lulu for long enough to clock my battle.

Like a flash, I was surrounded by eager men. They wanted to talk me through the fight. To advise the best way in around the rocks and pilings. To tell me how high to angle my rod. Where to stand and why. My dad even wanted to take my joke rod off me 'just to get the fish under control'. No way. Forget it, dad. They'd have needed heavy plant to free that stick from my grasp.

Finally, through a mixture of rod bending and hand-lining we managed to land a big fat ballans wrasse. A beauty. Full of reds and greens and bronze. With teeth like a gorilla.

I was proud of that fish. The men all nodded and patted my back and told me their own stories of big wrasse they'd caught. A few of them, my dad included, even wound in their far-cast baits to drop them down the edge.

Everyone that walked on the pier that afternoon came to admire my fish, as it lay on the concrete gasping its last gulps, slowly dying and drying in the sun. My mum and sisters turned up after going for a walk, or reading, or whatever it is girls and their mums do when men fish. Me, I was one of the men.

At the end of the day we all climbed into my dad's Ford Anglia, with me dearly clutching a very fat but very dead wrasse and a very broken toy fishing rod.

In the car, going back to our caravan, the sisters complained about the fish. It smelt. It was ugly. It had brown teeth and had brown stuff oozing out of it. I remember I asked my dad what we could do with it. What the next process was. Somehow, I thought we'd mount it or eat it or do something that immortalised it for ever.

Instead we stopped in a lay by and dad threw it onto a patch of drab sandy beach which was waiting for the tide. My last sight of the noble wrasse was a sad image. It looked dirty and out of place. Wasted. Dad told me it was alright, the gulls would eat it. I wanted this information to make me feel better, but deep down it didn't.

This was a beautiful day. A day chiselled into my memory wall. Full of pride and excitement and achievement. I felt like a man. I felt powerful and clever. But sad too.

In those days, everybody killed fish. No one ever
put fish back. I suppose we just assumed the seas were
full of them. We caught them and they were ours to
keep. Now, we know different. Now, I'm just happy
to borrow them. No, that's not true. These days I'm
HAPPIER just to borrow them. I'm sorry the wrasse
had to die. But he gave birth to something in me that I
don't think could now ever die.

A Rush Of Blood

By Ian Muckle

It all began for me when I was six years old, and little did I realise then that my first fish, a small but colourful perch of around half a pound from the Norfolk Broads, was to instil in me a fanaticism for the sport of angling which has never diminished, and that has led me into a semi-career of angling journalism. The annual family holiday in those days consisted of a boat vacation on the Broads, and from the time I was six until I reached the ripe old age of eleven, I spent many hours with my father catching bream, roach, rudd and perch from the mysterious reed-fringed waters. I can remember those days quite clearly - my father going out late at night to groundbait a swim and then, after a night with little sleep thanks to the excitement that a prospective day's fishing sent pulsing through my mind, creeping away with me in a dinghy during the early dawn hours.

Those were magic times, unforgettable times - the adrenalin pumping as the float disappeared and the unmistakable "breamy" smell from the bulging keepnet. Sharing those moments, the triumphs and disasters, with my father established a special bond between child and parent that has never lessened. Some forty years later, we still fish together, though now it is my turn to look after him instead of the other way round. What is more, we implanted that same enthusiasm for the sport in my two younger brothers, who are now constant angling companions. We were always going to be friends as well as brothers, but the love of angling and our childhood adventures pursuing our hobby strengthened that companionship into a close-knit tie.

If my father was the major influence in person in my youth, then a certain book was the main material force in formulating my angling future. I could almost quote "Mr Crabtree Goes Fishing", by Bernard Venables, from cover to cover; I drooled over those drawings of specimen fish. It seemed that the fish Mr Crabtree and Peter caught were always specimens, but I didn't care, and still recommend that volume to youngsters as something that they will find extremely readable and inspiring. In fact, though it was written so many years ago, it has recently been brought back into circulation, such has been the demand for it. So I was obviously not the only kid who pored through the pages of "Mr Crabtree" in wonderment.

As I progressed through my childhood years, the angling bug bit in many guises. When I moved to secondary school in West Lothian, I met up with a friend who shared the same passion, and many a memorable day we spent chasing the trout in Barbauchlaw Burn or Forrestfield Loch. In those days, we had not made the step into the finer arts of fly-fishing, and the humble worm or maggot or the spinner formed our main weaponry. Then came the sea angling phase, with the west coast of Scotland providing sport of a quality that is unlikely we will ever see again. I have many happy memories of my brother and I freezing and shivering under a January night sky as we searched the shore for cod; or those heady days spent with father and brother in our dinghy, afloat over a rich harvest of cod, haddock and whiting. Alas, thanks to the greed of the commercial boats, those days are long gone - but the nets can never erase the memories and the friendships shared. With the death of the west coast cod era, fly-fishing began to take over my life until nowadays, it dominates above all others, though I still enjoy all forms of angling, particularly boat fishing at sea.

All children dream of what the future will bring, and for younger anglers, these aspirations are usually of catching big fish or visiting exotic places with strange new species. Some of those dreams will come true, while some you will pursue all your life without realising them. But that's part of what angling is all about. I have been fortunate, and many of my childhood hopes have been satisfied. I've had some specimen fish and those which have left their indelible mark upon my mind -a 44lb cod from the Clyde coast; a 20lb plus rainbow trout; a 5lb 12oz brownie from glorious Loch Leven; and the 6lb haddock caught from the shore during a holiday, a fish that my brother and I gleefully ate before realising that it broke the British record for a shore caught fish by a mile! I've enjoyed angling in magnificent Florida, clad only in a pair of shorts and sneakers, and have added many new species to my tally, and some of them very memorable -a 7lb bonefish caught on fly down in the Keys; a 14lb snook that fought like a demon in the Gulf of Mexico; a 50lb cobia that took a light tackle offering from a boat in Tampa Bay; a 40lb tuna that reduced me to a physical wreck and almost made me wish I hadn't hooked it. The youthful fisherman must believe in his dreams, for surely some of them will be fulfilled.

In today's technological world, the progress made in fishing tackle has been astounding. But though decent gear is a bonus, a boy or girl can derive pleasure out of very mundane and ordinary rods and reels. I started off with a converted tank aerial and progressed to an old bamboo rod for my coarse fishing, while my first fly rod was an ancient greenheart that, on reflection, I just don't know how I managed to cast all day. But I did, and I loved it. I'm not criticising sophistication; it's almost necessary when you get older. However, it doesn't come cheap nowadays, and it's not essential for the sheer enjoyment of the sport. I do have to admit though, that it can make the young angler more proficient in a shorter time, and some would equate proficiency with greater satisfaction.

Based on my own experience, I would offer several pieces of advice to adults who intend introducing a girl or boy to angling. First of all, let them grow up understanding all aspects of the sport. It's not just about catching fish; it's also to do with learning to love and value the environment; to understand nature and its delicate balance; to respect the flora and fauna that are such a vital part of the hobby. Fly-fishing can be a difficult form of angling for the youngster to grasp, and quite frustrating when learning the game. It's important for the novice to actually hook and play a trout when first starting out. Take her or him to one of the well stocked small waters which are to be found all over the country. I operate as an instructor at one of our Scottish stillwaters, and we have an arrangement by which on the last afternoon of instruction, the pupils are allowed to fish a specially stocked pool where they are almost guaranteed to catch, no matter how poor their technique. Once they have experienced the thrill of that first trout on light tackle, they will be hooked for life. Finally, make sure they take one of the regular publications relevant to their branch of the sport. These carry regular advice for juniors, most having their own special page.

A final thought - I often find myself sitting on a quiet evening in the boat on my favourite Loch Leven, when my mind drifts back to those boyhood days on the Norfolk Broads, when I was only learning the trade and waiting for the bob of a coloured float. I can still feel that rush of adrenalin when the float disappeared - you never forget!

A Marvel Of Caddis

An extract from
'The Angler's Sedge'

By Taff Price

The birthplace of the stream was high up in the hills, just a syrup slow trickle emanating from the soft bog, a wetness from the spongy sphagnum moss. In that place it dampened the sundew and wetted the feet of the snipe and curlew.

Small trickle joined small trickle and slowly gathered strength until they found a tiny brook. Over thousands of years this small stream had carved itself a deep valley in the Pre-Cambrian granite, a valley flanked by moss covered oaks and bushes of wild bilberry, where the buzzard nested and where owls slept the daylight hours. A valley where stray sheep went to hide from the rest of the world and where small boys discovered new worlds. Perhaps in earlier times it was a much bigger stream, a legacy of the ice age when the melting glaciers retreated before the warming sun. The stream flowed through this wooded valley a place scented by wild mint, wilder garlic. Small trout hid behind the stones and green frogs sat goggled eyed in the green of the bankside, maybe they were drugged by the peppermint or the scent of the garlic. For a short while the singing stream left behind all the natural beauty and gushed through a large, rust red iron pipe. It had been easier in those days to carry the road over an iron pipe rather than construct a bridge. It next flowed through a park we called "Fairy Glen", still alive it sang its way towards the sea, ignoring the fact that careless man had constructed the town's rubbish dump a hundred yards or so to the left.

The place was a mass of grey, white and black, as gulls aided by hump backed crows picked over the waste like Victorian scavengers. Soon it reached the sandbanks where it slid quietly between the mounds of shifting sands and close, rabbit clipped grass. Once again it flowed into a large iron pipe, this time a pipe encrusted with barnacles, bearded with seaweed and scoured by limpets; from the mouth of this pipe it poured its soul into the Irish Sea.

It must be well over forty years ago since I sat by the side of that stream, on a carpet of grass and clover, but I can remember it as though it were only yesterday; it was my introduction to the world of the caddis or the sedge as some people called it. I can recall vividly staring in wonder into the water, marvelling at the tiny, gravel encrusted caddis larvae busying themselves in the silt of the stream.

It is strange why I should remember that insignificant stream and its tiny inhabitants, but even today when I see a fluttering sedge or a tiny caddis larva, I remember that small boy who sat beside a stream just looking at the insects that crawled midst the gravel. I would like to tell you that the stream still sings in the valley on its way to the sea but alas it is long gone. Someone has taken the water for another valley and another place and the dry stones of the stream lie like the skeleton of some giant reptile, dry and bleached by time. Herons now tiptoe on the sphagnum so as not to wake the spirits of the dead stream. No longer do the caddis busy themselves in the silt and neither do the brown winged sedge flies flutter above the sandbanks. They remain only as a crystal of memory in my mind, a small spark that rekindles, no matter where I am, whenever I see a sedge flying at dusk.

Like Father Like Son

By Tom Saville

We were always a fishing family. My father was a reasonably keen angler, and although he was a gruff, stern disciplinarian who thought that a clip on the ear and banishment to the bedroom was a suitable punishment for the slightest misdemeanour (as many fathers did in the '20s and '30s) he lost no time in taking me fishing with him as soon as he felt I was old enough. Ten years old, in fact. It was quite noticeable, even to my young mind, that whenever we fished together he was kindness itself, with never a cross word. We were fishing pals.

We lived in a Cheshire village, with a lake and a canal within walking distance of home. I don't recall much fishing pressure on the lake, and it was easy to find a secluded spot at the waterside. At first, I wasn't allowed to actually fish. I had to watch dad and be instructed in the intricacies of tying knots in Jagut, nipping split shot on the line in the correct places, making bread paste (with a lovely aniseed smell), sticking a tiny hook into the right end of a wriggling maggot, and all the other things involved in stillwater coarse fishing. After two or three sessions, I couldn't stand this any longer, and pestered him for my own outfit. The result was my proud ownership of a little cane rod, tiny brass centrepin reel loaded with cuttyhunk line, two floats (porcupine and peacock quills), a rattling tin of split shot, and a few gold hooks-to-gut.

Bait was easy to get - even if the "Saturday penny" pocket money was spent on sweets and not maggots, there was bread in the pantry and worms to be dug from the nearby muck-heap.

Thinking back, it must have been the combination of the peace and quiet of the surroundings, the excitement of catching the fish, and above all the feeling of "togetherness" with my father, which engendered the passion for fishing which is still with me.

When my own son, John arrived, it was natural for me to lose no time in introducing him to the joys of angling. By that time, I had moved to Nottinghamshire, and had graduated from the meres and lakes of Cheshire with their roach, perch and bream, to the trout filled rivers of Derbyshire and the art of casting a fly. I had joined a trout-fishing club in Ashbourne, with fishing on two brooks, both tributaries of the Dove.

And so it was at the tender age of six, despite opinions voiced by others that he was much too young, John was initiated into the skills of fly-fishing. I gave him a little six-foot split cane fly rod, a cheap reel and a well used silk line, some of the new nylon casts and a few of my home-tied flies.

In spite of his lack of years, or perhaps because of it, he quickly learned the basics of the overhead cast. The most difficult part was getting him to wait long enough for the line to extend fully behind him before making the forward cast. Kids are always too impatient.

The lightweight rod was ideal for his lack of strength, and its short length offered no leverage to tire his arm muscles. The rod was also an ideal model for fishing the tiny, often overgrown, Henmore Brook, and when I knew that he could cast well enough to catch a trout, that is where I took him for his first fishing session.

The Henmore is only five or six metres wide, but it is a typical trout stream in miniature, with pools and runs and weed-beds waving in the current. Although there were many stretches where the banks were lined with alder bushes, several more open parts were suitable for John's limited abilities. I can see him now in my mind's eye, trotting along the bank in his little green wellies, rod pointing backwards over his shoulder as instructed ("You won't break the tip by running into a tree, John, if you carry it that way."), and scaring every trout in the process.

"Keep well back from the water until you're ready to cast to a fish. Trout are very scary, and if one sees you it will scoot away and hide. You have to creep along quietly so that the fish can't see you. You mustn't jump about or stamp your feet because that will scare the fish too," I told him. Surprisingly, for he was a mischievous and rather wilful child, he did as he was told, and the trout of the Henmore were able to resume their peaceful existence, for a time at least.

Before long, we came to a spot where there was enough space for a short back-cast, and a spherical

shaped hawthorn bush on our bank gave sufficient
cover. We crept on our knees and hid behind the bush.
Two seconds later, I heard the plop of a rising trout.
We both poked one eye round the bush. The widening
rings were right in the middle of the stream, an easy
cast even for a six-year old.

The line was well greased - this was before the days
of self-floating plastic fly lines - with a 7 foot tapered
nylon leader looped to the end. A hackled Greenwell's
Glory dry fly, chosen by me as a possible tempter of
John's first trout, was knotted on and anointed with
Mucilin floatant. Another "plop" announced that the
trout was still feeding. We were a couple of yards
downstream from its position.

"Peep round the bush carefully and see exactly
where he makes a ring on the water."

Plop. Exactly opposite a clump of bushes on the
other bank. An enthusiastic rise to an olive dun. I pulled
two or three yards of line out of the rod tip.

"I can do that, Dad," he objected.

"O.K. Just thought I'd help."

"I want to do it myself."

"Right. You remember what I told you about false
casting? Keep the line in the air and pull a bit more off
the reel each time. Then when you think the line is
long enough, try and drop the fly in the middle of the
stream a bit further past that clump of dark grassy stuff

that's growing on the other side. Then it will float over the fish and with a bit of luck he'll see it and grab it."

Miraculously, everything went right. The fly didn't splash on the water during the false-casting (I must have taught him properly), his aim was spot on and the trout came up and took the fly with a solid splash.

"Strike!" I yelled, but there was really no need. The fish bolted upstream and hooked itself. Before I could do anything, John was reeling furiously, rod tip high in the air, and a seven-inch brownie was lifted from the water, turning cartwheels in the air. John swung the fish onto the bank and pounced on it like a cat on a mouse. His face was a picture. I had instilled in him the fact that fish can't feel pain like people can, so his sole feeling was one of supreme pleasure. He had done everything right. His very first fish was beautiful in his hands.

"Let's put it back," I whispered. The trout slid slowly from John's hands and with a flick of the tail was gone.

We exchanged grins. But there was a lot more to it than that . . .

Jack Sharp

By Bernard Cribbins

Someone once said that the first fish that most anglers
catch is a perch and certainly they are very
accommodating creatures when approached by a small
boy with a bent pin and a worm, but my first fish were
sticklebacks.

I come from Oldham, in Lancashire and my fishing
began with a net and a jam jar in the local ponds and
streams, especially a place called Hollow Brook. This
was an overflow from a reservoir on the edge of the
Penines. Part of it ran underground in a tunnel about
six feet high. This was a great place for large sticklebacks
or "Jack Sharps" as we called them.

Then one day I saw one of my mates with a rod
and line complete with a red-topped float and a real
hook! Well that was the end of the net wasn't it - off it
came and tied on the cane was a length of cotton thread
with two spent matches tied on as a float. I didn't have
a hook and somehow a bent pin detracted from the
delicacy of the outfit, so I came up with the idea of
tying the worm on. It was an unqualified success! The
worm was heavy enough to cock the "float" and the
very best bit was catching TWO sticklebacks at the
same time - one on each end of the worm! The hardest
part was getting the worm to keep still long enough to
get a slip knot round its middle - that was more fun
than fishing!

It was about this time that my mate Jack Rigby
and I became professionals. We had heard that a man

who had an old porcelain sink in his back yard, which he used as a pond for goldfish, was in the market for new stock. So we arrived at his home with jam jars full of prime, red-breasted tiddlers. I seem to remember he was a bit amazed at the sight of these two scruffy kids with fishing rods and loaded jam jars - but he said he'd have them and we got sixpence between us - a fortune in those days.

Not long after this, Jack and I graduated to fishing for gudgeon in Alexandra Park Lake with more sophisticated tackle bought for twopence. This was a cotton line, a piece of peacock quill for a float and a hook to gut, with a couple of lead shot - complete with winder. With this and a slightly longer cane we were able to reach over the railings round the lake; with bread paste for bait the gudgeon didn't stand a chance! The only trouble with fishing the park lake was that a certain large policeman called Bobby Finney would suddenly appear from nowhere. He was a huge man and I'm sure a totally benevolent, old-fashioned bobby, but we never found out his views on the finer points of the "Gentle Art" because we were too busy legging it to the exit trailing fishing rods, bait and various other bits and pieces in our wake.

It seems that around this time a lot of my fishing was illegal - I remember that some very good carp and goldfish could be caught in the mill lodges alongside the many cotton mills, which were the main industry

of Oldham at that time. These lodges were small
reservoirs that supplied the water for the mill boilers
and the recycling system meant the water was warm
and the fish thrived. There always seemed to be a gap
in the railings and one could squeeze through and fish
very happily until someone started shouting to clear
us out or until the dreaded cry went up, "Cops are
coming!"

My younger sister Kathleen was a very good
lookout - she was quite small and nippy and once we
got her trained to SAS standards she was invaluable.
I'm quite sure that it was all this early speed training
that helped her to become a good hockey player and
captain of the town netball team.

My fishing since those days has covered coarse, game
and sea - from sticklebacks to sharks, taking in on the

way salmon and trout and the lovely grayling - bass in the surf in November on Irish beaches, when one day was summer and the next cold and grey with driving snow flurries - rainbow trout 10,000 feet up in the mountains of Ethiopia - Nile perch and tiger fish in Lake Chamo whilst dodging hippos - stingrays and squid on the jetties of Glenelg near Adelaide - chub on the fly at the bottom of the garden - and blissful days on the Test and Kennet learning about chalkstream fishing from my good friend John Goddard.

It is a wonderful sport, art, pastime - call it what you will - and I'm forever grateful to those bristling, red-breasted little warriors - the sticklebacks!

All In The Genes

By Tony Pawson

Hundreds of millions of people all over the world enjoy fishing. It is the main participator sport in countries as different as Japan and America, Australia and Canada. In Britain and Ireland over four million fish because it is an inborn instinct in so many of us. As that great philosopher of fishing, Lord Grey, wrote: "To enjoy fishing to the full a person must be born an angler. The passion may be latent, for years it may not discover itself owing to lack of opportunity, but, if it is not revealed when opportunity comes, it is not there."

The greatest good fortune of my life was that both I and my son John have that instinct and had early opportunity to discover it. Instinct, as Darwin commented, is as important to man, as to the rest of the animal kingdom, though overlaid by "Civilisation". For the very young instinct happily reigns supreme. When, aged four, I peered over a bridge after a three mile walk to the Tullich burn in Scotland it was instinct that made me thrill to the whispering waters below. There was a special fascination as the current now clouded the surface, now left a clear window of sight to the stones at the bottom. With beating heart I dropped my worm into the mysterious depths and thrilled to the gentle tug on the line. The instinctive reaction and the sight of a small trout sailing over my head into the heather was excitement enough to confirm that fishing would always be a main strand of my life.

That trout was my first fish landed, but the first one hooked was at the other end of the weight scale and a near disaster. My father was in the Sudan Civil service and earlier that year I had been out there and taken to watch some fishing at one of the dams on the vast Nile river. Some of the fish there were of appropriate size for such a huge river with Nile perch running up to four hundred pounds or so. As one of the party went to his car he gave me his line to hold and a minute later one of these monsters seized hold and I was towed into the river before letting go. So I claim that the first fish I hooked was so large it caught me!

That first fish is always a memorable occasion as was my first trout on an artificial fly a year later. Then there was the excitement of my first sea-trout caught unexpectedly in the Coulags burn, where it had run up from the Carron river. For a fly fisherman the really special event however is that first salmon. When you are young, joy and sadness are more keenly felt, and the pain of losing a fish is bitter indeed. Before the joy of a salmon caught, I had to experience the heartache of one lost. On the Dawrus river in Ireland aged eight I was left with the kindly ghillie, James Meehan, while my father and elder brother fished ahead. They both ignored a small pool where a racing foam-flecked current brought a touch of white to the brown spate water.

"Could I catch anything here?" I asked James.

"Sure you might. Then you mightn't. But if you did it would be a sea-trout."

A sea-trout was prize enough for me and I kept working the fly deep and fast. While movement attracts sea-trout, salmon, like the fly moved slow. Perhaps the eddy into which the fly swirled held it still for a moment. Certainly there came the immovable resistance, then the stately surge of a salmon. The trout rod, and limited line on the trout reel, were strained to their limits; the fast current aided the fish. At last there was the sizeable salmon, beaten, floating on its side towards the waiting net. Then my heart broke as the hold gave, the small fly snapped out. How could it be so near and not landed? How cruel to win the difficult battle then still be cheated of the prize.

Fish lost often stay longer in the memory than those landed, and that is still sharply in focus more than sixty years later. But so too is the joy of a salmon caught a few years later. This was on the nearby Erriff river in a pool where again I was expecting only sea-trout and had already caught several. Then came the great swirl at the fly and a racing fight before my first salmon was finally in the net. Such was my happiness that I stopped fishing and sat waiting, hugging myself with pleasure until I could show my prize to my father and brother who were fishing down towards me from the upper reaches.

My own fishing when young had largely been a learning by doing process with my father fishing a different river and the ghillie or my mother looking after my brother and myself as we fished the burns. The snag with the Tullich and the Coulags was that both had eels as well as trout and if an eel took the worm it would spin round and round tangling the cast. Mother hated touching them and if we caught one would cut the cast off and march us home to the fisherman's cottage where we stayed. So at least we learnt to avoid hooking eels, though sometimes that led to the owner taking us out into the bay to set night lines. Then in the morning we could watch enthralled as sea fish of varying shapes and sizes began to appear, white and ethereal in the green of the water before being revealed as codlings or plaice, or dogfish or flounders.

My son John was also an instinctive fisherman and like me was enthralled with it by the time he was four. One incident proved that beyond doubt. I was fishing the Spey while my wife looked after John and my daughter, Sarah, aged six and five. They were at the edge of a field where a bank went down to the riverside. On that hot summer day, flies began to plague a herd of young bullocks, who suddenly stampeded at the three of them. Hilarie, my wife, seized Sarah and pulled her under the bank for protection, shouting for John to run for cover. He also dashed down the bank, but only to throw himself on the salmon I had just caught, and left on the shingle, in order to save it from the bullocks; an instinctive angler from his earliest days and with a proper sense of priorities.

John started fishing aged four, helped by his three year old sister. Worm fishing for trout was an ideal beginning as it was for me, but John was an instinctive artificial fly-fisher from the start and adverse to the act of putting a worm on a hook. Not so Sarah, who dutifully threaded them on for him. For both of them, the float had magnetic attraction, keeping concentration intense, making the excitement tangible as it dipped suddenly under the surface. One of John's first fish, on the Onny river in Shropshire, just above its junction with the Teme, was a chub of near two pounds, and joy was unconfined.

John was only seven when he hooked his first salmon in an equally unlikely pool. It was my first day on Sutherland's Brora river, and while I never like having a ghillie myself I had hired one for the day to look after John, so that I could try out the river without having to devote time to helping him. We walked up past the coal-mine at the bottom, which had been going to close until the miners bought and worked it themselves. We fished on up for pool after pool, then fished back towards the car.

In mid-afternoon, I had a lively salmon and by then was far ahead of John and the ghillie. Walking back to find them I was immediately aware of an excited hubbub. Set to fish a small pool where the casting was easier, but the salmon rarely if ever caught, John had done just that. His fly, forcefully cast double-handed into the gentle run, had been just as forcefully seized. Only at the end of the fight did the ghillie give some assistance and he, and I were nearly as excited as John. But no one and nothing can match the excitement of a first fly-caught salmon at that age.

Rather than continue to inculcate him in my own bad habits once he graduated to fly-fishing at the age of six, I ensured that he had a week's proper instruction at the Abu centre at Aviemore. Having myself been brought up to concentrate solely on fly-fishing, it was my belief that you should also learn to spin. That, too, he was correctly taught here. It so happened that the week provided the best salmon fishing I had ever had, and John missed most of it. That has proved small loss compared to the vast advantage of learning good habits and correct method right at the start of a fly-fishing career.

The importance of proper training at a young age was underlined by John's subsequent development into a remarkably expert fly fisherman who has not only won the world fly-fishing championship in Tasmania in 1988, but has been the only member of all three winning England world cup teams in the last seven years against some twenty other countries, as well as having outstanding success in other national, home international and European events and, more importantly, a vast enjoyment of his ordinary fishing worldwide.

One For The Rod

By Tom Quinn

We had taken the train from London down to Salisbury that morning to fish the Avon. This was in those heady pre-abstraction days in the late 1960s when trout fishing that far down the river was still pretty good and tickets were to be had at prices we youngsters could afford.

The fishing hadn't been up to much, so at lunchtime, my friends and I repaired to the pub. My acquaintance with alcohol was slight, but I drank with enthusiasm and then rolled and staggered back down towards the river, shouting at trees and abusing the poor sad cattle. My friends sprawled around lazily behind me on the lush banks of the river but, despite my condition, I put up a rod and began to fish.

I was so drunk that the motion of the rod seemed to impart itself to the whole of my body. When the rod went back, so did I. When it went forward I followed it. I swayed back and forth quite happily for some time and then, while striving for that perfect cast, my rod went forward a little further than it should and I followed it, into the river. I splashed my way to the surface, cursing and swearing. The Avon still had a good, strong flow at that time and I sailed away towards Fordingbridge before striking out for the shore some thirty yards downstream. I dragged myself up through the rushes and lay gasping at the water's edge for some time. My friends could be seen stuffing grass into their mouths in a vain attempt to stop themselves laughing. We lit a fire and, in full view of countless innocent cattle and ramblers, I removed my trousers and propped them up on a stick close to the flames.

Undaunted by my white knees and red and white striped shorts, a few fish had started to rise and I wandered the banks happily in pursuit of them. My friends, a little recovered from their apoplexy, did the same.

Imagine then my sorrow when, on returning to collect my trousers I discovered that they had long ago fallen into the unguarded fire. I managed to salvage one turn-up and the major part of one leg, but this was little consolation when I found myself standing at Salisbury station smelling like a musty mackerel and surrounded by the stern, staring women of the town. Dogs barked at me and children jeered as I boarded the train and I was convinced for a while that the guard would make me travel in the van. In the event he took pity on me and I travelled the up train a sadder and wiser youth.

My First Day Fishing

By Michaela

One day on a Saturday I was going fishing with my dad. My dad set up the rods and put a maggot on the hook. I was sitting on the deckchair with the legs folded up and I fell in the water but it was shallow. My dad had to take me home to get changed but I still went fishing. I sat there for five hours and I hadn't caught anything. I was bored and dad was catching every five minutes. He caught a big fish. He was going home at six o'clock and I had to wait for two hours.

"Dad," I said, "can I go home because I'm bored."
He said, "Okay."
I told my mum about the fishing and I still go today.

A Block Off The Old Chip

By Peter Lapsley

My sixth birthday is etched indelibly into my memory
for it brought with it my first set of fishing tackle.

Why father should have given it to me, I have no
idea. He was no angler himself at the time. Perhaps he
simply bought it on an impulse. Whatever the reason,
it was the most inspired present he could have found me.

It was as simple an affair as can be imagined - the
rod consisted of two lengths of bamboo cane with tin
ferrules, wire rings and a rudimentary handle. The
plastic reel was loaded with a length of nylon (a new
fangled material in those days). And the whole kaboodle
was mounted on a garishly printed sheet of cardboard
along with a dozen split shot, two gilt hooks to nylon
and a beautiful quill float with a red tip. It probably
came from Woolworths. It was pure magic. I gazed at
it all day.

Fortunately, my birthday falls on 19th June, three
days after the opening of the coarse fishing season.

When father came home from work, he asked
whether, as a birthday treat, I wanted to go swimming
or fishing. What a silly question!

Having dug some worms, we clambered into the
car and headed off along the north Norfolk lanes to a
disused gravel pit he had spotted some time previously.

At the edge of the pit was a collapsed wartime pill-
box, its thick, grey concrete roof sloping down towards
the inkiness of water. We assembled my tackle, impaled
a worm on the hook and cast probably no more than

about ten feet out. As father turned and started walking back towards the car to collect his cigarettes, the red tipped float righted itself, subsided into the glassy surface and slid from view.

"The float's gone," I yelled.

"Don't worry," he said, "we've probably got too many shot on the line. Just pull it out and we'll take one off."

I started reeling in. The rod bent and shuddered slightly, and up from the depths came the most beautiful fish you have ever seen - a roach, six inches long, gleaming silver in the evening sunshine, its pinky-orange fins like translucent rose petals. We tapped it on the head and I laid it out beside me on a clean, white napkin.

As we fished on that first evening of my fishing life, a photographer appeared, a freelance who sold his pictures to the local press. He took a photograph of me fishing from the old pill-box, and it appeared later in East Anglian life. I hope and believe that my father may have it still, tucked away among the family snaps in his loft.

I ate that first roach when we got home, fried in butter, carefully picking out countless needle-like bones from amongst the clean white flesh. It was delicious.

We caught dozens of little roach at that gravel pit, and perch and eels, too, and we loved the place. Imagine our dismay , then, when the owner turned up one day and said that it was, in fact, a nature reserve, and that he could not allow us to fish there. Whether people in general were kinder in the late 1940s than they are now, or whether he was simply a generous and sympathetic man, I cannot say. But he directed us to a mill stream half a mile away, which he also owned, and said we could fish there as often as we wished. We did. I hope father offered suitable apologies and thanks.

When we moved down to Watford in the early 1950s, I continued my fishing on the Grand Union Canal, hell bent on breaking the British gudgeon record which stands then and stands now at 4ozs 4dms.

Since then, I have fished for perch, roach, rudd, tench, carp, barbel, bream and pike both here and in Germany; for trout, first on the little river Chess in Hertfordshire and then on rivers, lakes and lochs and reservoirs throughout the British Isles; for grayling both in the chalk streams of southern England and on marvellous spate rivers in the north; for sea trout wherever I have been able to find them and as far afield as the Falkland islands; for cod, bass, mullet, dabs and pollack in the Wash, the Thames Estuary, off the south coast and from Devon beaches; and for weird, wonderful, sometimes huge and often hideous sea fish in Guyana, Aden and the Arabian Gulf.

Today, I am privileged to be a member of that club that has three miles of the most exquisite chalk stream fishing you can imagine, beautifully kept, its water crystal clear, its trout fit, fat and fussy. But I am very glad I started my fishing the way I did.

Simple coarse fishing taught me more about fish, the water in which they live and the ways in which they behave than I could ever have learnt by other means. It was cheap (free!), so I could do lots of it - all day, every day, through every weekend and holiday, except during the close season or when mother dragged me off, protesting, to watch the changing of the guard or somesuch. And it gave me a sense of values. I am sure I would not prize, as I do, a half pound roach, a gudgeon a third that size or a fierce little brownie from a moorland stream had I started my fishing in pursuit of stocked rainbows weighing in at two pounds or more apiece.

Having started me off, father fished hardly at all until he retired in the mid-1970s. So I built him a rod, bought him a reel and a fly line, tied him a few flies and faced him in roughly the right direction. Now, twenty years on, frailer and less mobile than he was, he still heads for the waterside twice a week through spring, summer and autumn, enjoys his days in the open and catches his share of trout. It has been enormous fun being able to give him back some of the pleasure he has given me. He has become a "block off the old chip", as you might say.

Dougie's Tench

By Chris Yates

It was rather late in the year when Dougie arrived at the village pond for his first attempt at fishing. He'd just been given a new rod and reel for his eighth birthday and was obviously keen to see if they performed as well by the waterside as they had done in his garden. But it was November, the weather was cold and I warned him that fish in small ponds can often seem to vanish completely in the winter.

We assembled on the bank after I'd collected Dougie from school, along with my own two children, Camilla (8) and Alex (5). I had to promise Dougie's mother that I wouldn't let him fall in and that I'd bring him home before dark. Camilla and Alex were experienced anglers in their own right, so I left them to tackle up while I helped Dougie with his own sparkling new gear.

"Have you got your own hooks?" I asked as I threaded the line through the rings of his flashy carbon rod.

"Yes," he said, producing a little tin box from his pocket.

"I've got this three-er."

"What's a three-er?" I asked, thinking I was obviously not keeping abreast of modern tackle developments. Dougie carefully picked out a large treble hook and proudly handed it over to me.

"Ah," I said, "actually, this is only for big pike and there aren't even any little pike in this pond. We'll use something more suitable."

Dougie looked doubtfully at the size 12 barbless that I tied onto his line.

"But that's only a one-er!" he protested.

Eventually all our floats were sitting pert, colourful and expectant on the dark water. I tossed in a few squeezed bits of breadflake and we stood quietly watching for the fish to come home for tea.

After a few minutes, three local lads, Mark, Philip and Greg arrived on their bicycles. Seeing us with our rods, looking so eager they obviously guessed that great things were about to happen and immediately pedalled home for their rods. Soon there were six floats decorating the margins of the village pond, and even if Dougie didn't have any luck I thought he might at least see someone else get something.

However, for the first hour, Dougie didn't really mind what happened. Here he was at last, really fishing. Furthermore, he was fishing alongside boys and a girl who, according to local legend, had actually caught genuine, authentic fish - fish with colours and shapes that he'd admired in books, but which he'd never seen in reality - fish with important names, like carp, roach and tench.

Now there was every likelihood that he'd see and maybe even touch one of these magical creatures himself. Perhaps he'd even catch one. He'd thought initially, that someone would get something straight away, despite my reservations about the conditions, but the afternoon was sinking quickly into the short November evening and none of the floats had even twitched. There had been no movement on the surface at all, apart from the slow drifting of yellow fallen leaves. But Dougie had listened to the stories that Camilla had told him at school, about all the great fish she'd seen and caught, so he knew those marvellous things were down there, lurking mysteriously in the depths. There was probably one right beneath his float.

"My feet are getting cold!" complained Alex.
"I can hardly see my float any more," said Mark.
"Anyone had a bite yet?" asked Philip.
"No!" they all chorused.

It was only the communal enthusiasm that kept everyone going so long, but as it began to get darker and colder their keenness gradually lost its edge, to be replaced by a general longing for a fireside chair and a hot cup of cocoa. Also, there was that promise I'd made to Dougie's mum about bringing him home dry before dark. But he was the only one who didn't want to pack up.

"Last cast then," I said.

"Here, we'll take the float off your line and you can feel for a bite. We can't see anything much anyway. Also, I'll re-bait with something different."

Down at the bottom of my creel was the remains of a black pudding that I'd been trying on the river for chub and barbel (with some success). Perhaps the fish in the pond might appreciate something spicy and meaty on this cold winter evening. I moulded a small piece on Dougie's hook and flicked it into the margins.

"What happens if I get a bite?" asked Dougie as I handed back his rod.

"Just gently hold the line above the reel and when it goes tight jerk the rod up sharpish - but not too hard."

While he stood patiently waiting, I helped Alex untangle his line and put Camilla's rod safely in the back of our car. Though Alex was also having one last cast, Camilla had done enough fishing for the day.

"My fingers are freezing!" she whined. "I'll sit in the car and wait."

The three village lads started reeling in and putting their away their gear. Mark came over to me and suggested we wait for milder weather before we cast again. He was interrupted by Dougie who suddenly said,

"I think I've got one!"

But he was standing so still and his rod seemed so inanimate that no one believed him. However, the reason he wasn't moving was because he was paralysed with shock and the reason his rod wasn't bent was because he was pointing it directly at a firmly pulling fish.

I crouched down so that I could see the rod silhouetted against the dark sky and it jerked quite violently, with the tip suddenly curving to the left.

"He has got one!" I said.

Everyone began running towards us, all yelling and shouting. Camilla heard the commotion, burst out of the car and came dashing back down the bank to see what the matter was. Of course this was quite unsettling to Dougie.

Consider his predicament: after much waiting, dreaming and hoping he'd finally made miraculous contact with the mythical underwater world, but nothing had quite prepared him for this. He was stunned. Furthermore, it was dark and he couldn't see what was happening. Also the entire world of experienced anglers was shouting in his ears, giving incomprehensible advice;

"Let him run!"

"Give it sidestrain!"

"Steer it away from the weedbeds!"

"Let it swim round in circles!"

It was Dougie's head that was going round in circles, but he didn't lose it altogether and by raising the rod steadily higher, he eventually managed to bring the unseen fish up to the surface.

It splashed excitingly and kept splashing as Dougie began to walk backwards, attempting to drag it up the bank and onto dry land. I saw a pale flank glimmering in the margins and reaching down, got a firm grip round it and hoisted it ashore. (Someone had moved the net and we couldn't find it in the dark, in all the kerfuffle).

"Well done, Dougie," I said. "You've got a tench."

"Cor!" said Alex, "a big one."

"The only fish of the day," said Mark, "and you caught it."

"Your mummy won't mind us being late now," said Camilla.

There was just enough glow left in the late evening sky for us to discern the tench's small fine scales and its beautifully rounded fins and tail, but we couldn't see any of its subtle greens and golds. I carefully unhooked it and handed it to Dougie, who held it in silent reverence for a moment, before gently releasing it. He was still too overwhelmed to say anything but he was also obviously very happy.

We piled into the car and set off home, every one of us a true angler now.

Dougie had been confirmed by a half pound-tench.